Adobe® Audition™ 1.5

Classroom in a Book®

Property of:
Matthew Hinds
Matt's Music

Adobe

www.adobepress.com

© 2005 Adobe Systems Incorporated. All rights reserved.

Adobe® Audition™ 1.5 Classroom in a Book

This book, as well as the software described in it, is furnished under license and may be used or copied only in accordance with the terms of such license. The content of this book is furnished for informational use only, is subject to change without notice, and should not be construed as a commitment by Adobe Systems Incorporated. Adobe Systems Incorporated assumes no responsibility or liability for any errors or inaccuracies that may appear in this book.

Except as permitted by such license, no part of this book may be reproduced, stored in a retrieval system, or transmitted, in any form or by any means, electronic, mechanical, recording, or otherwise, without the prior written permission of Adobe Systems Incorporated.

Please remember that existing artwork, movies, sounds, or images that you may want to include in your project may be protected under copyright law. The unauthorized incorporation of such material into your new work could be a violation of the rights of the copyright owner. Please be sure to obtain any permission required from the copyright owner.

Any references to company names or individual names in sample templates and other project files are for demonstration purposes only and are not intended to refer to any actual organization or person.

Adobe, the Adobe logo, the Adobe Press logo, Adobe Audition, Adobe Premiere, and Adobe After Effects are either registered trademarks or trademarks of Adobe Systems Incorporated in the United States and/or other countries. Microsoft, Windows, and Windows NT are registered trademarks of Microsoft Corporation in the U.S. and/or other countries. MPEG Layer 3 audio compression technology is licensed by Fraunhofer IIS and Thompson. mp3PRO audio coding technology licensed from Coding Technologies, Fraunhofer IIS and Thomson Multimedia. All other trademarks are the property of their respective owners.

Supply of this product does not convey a license nor imply any right to distribute mp3-encoded or mp3PRO-encoded data created with this product in revenue-generating broadcast systems (terrestrial, satellite, cable, and/or other distribution channels), streaming applications (via Internet, intranets and/or other networks), other content-distribution systems (pay-audio or audio-on-demand applications and the like) or on physical media (compact discs, digital versatile discs, semiconductor chips, hard drives, memory cards and the like). An independent license for such use is required. For details, please visit http://www.mp3licensing.com

Contains an implementation of the LZW algorithm licensed under U.S. Patent 4,558,302.

Notice to U.S. government end users. The software and documentation are "Commercial Items," as that term is defined at 48 C.F.R. §2.101, consisting of "Commercial Computer Software" and "Commercial Computer Software Documentation," as such terms are used in 48 C.F.R. §12.212 or 48 C.F.R §227.7202, as applicable. Consistent with 48 C.F.R. §12.212 or 48 C.F.R. §§227.7202-1 through 227.7202-4, as applicable, the Commercial Computer Software and Commercial Computer Software Documentation are being licensed to U.S. Government end users (a) only as Commercial items and (b) with only those rights as are granted to all other end users pursuant to the terms and condition herein. Unpublished-rights reserved under the copyright laws of the United States. Adobe Systems Incorporated, 345 Park Avenue, San Jose, CA 94110-2704, USA. For U.S. Government End Users, Adobe agrees to comply with all applicable equal opportunity laws including, if appropriate, the provisions of Executive Order 11246, as amended, Section 402 of the Vietnam Era Veterans Readjustment Assistance Act of 1974 (38 USC 4212), and Section 503 of the Rehabilitation Act of 1973, as amended, and the regulations at 41 CFR Parts 60-1 through 60-60, 60-250, and 60-741. The affirmative action clause and regulations contained in the preceding sentence shall be incorporated by reference.

Adobe Press books are published by Peachpit Press, Berkeley, California 94710.
For the latest on Adobe Press books go to www.adobepress.com
To report errors, please send a note to errata@peachpit.com.

ISBN 0-321-26793-1

Printed in the U.S.A.

9 8 7 6 5 4 3 2 1

Contents

Getting Started

Welcome to Adobe® Audition. Audition is a powerful audio editing and production tool that offers precision, control, and seamless integration with other Adobe professional software including Adobe Premiere Pro and Adobe After Effects. Using Audition, you can produce professional-quality sound files for distribution electronically, on CD or DVD or for other recording purposes.

About Classroom in a Book

Adobe Audition 1.5 Classroom in a Book® is part of the official training series for Adobe audio and video software from Adobe Systems, Inc.

The lessons are designed so that you can learn at your own pace. If you're new to Adobe Audition, you'll learn the fundamentals you'll need to master to put the program to work. If you've already been using Adobe Audition, you'll find that Classroom in a Book teaches many advanced features, including tips and techniques for using this exciting audio tool.

Each lesson provides step-by-step instructions for creating a specific project. You can follow the book from start to finish, or do only the lessons that meet your interests and needs. Each lesson concludes with a review section summarizing what you've covered.

Prerequisites

Before beginning to use *Adobe Audition 1.5 Classroom in a Book*, you should have a working knowledge of your computer and its operating system. Make sure you know how to use the mouse and standard menus and commands, and also how to open, save, and close files. The lessons reference the file extensions when describing file names. You can set Windows to display or not display file extensions. If you need to review these techniques, see the printed or online documentation included with your Microsoft Windows documentation.

Installing the program

You must purchase the Adobe Audition software separately. For complete instructions on installing the software, see the "How to Install" Readme file on the application CD.

Copying the Classroom in a Book files

The Classroom in a Book CD includes folders containing all the electronic files for the lessons. Each lesson has its own folder. You must install these folders on your hard disk to use the files for the lessons. To save room on your hard disk, you can install the folders for each lesson as you need them.

1 Insert the Adobe Audition Classroom in a Book CD into your CD-ROM drive. The CD contains both data and music tracks. If your computer is set to automatically play music CDs, you may need to access the lesson folders using Windows by closing any multimedia applications such as Windows Media Player or iTunes.

2 Create a folder on your hard disk and name it AA_CIB.

3 Do one of the following:

• Copy the individual lesson folders into the AA_CIB folder.

• Copy only the single lesson folder you need.

Additional resources

Adobe Audition 1.5 Classroom in a Book is not meant to replace documentation that comes with the program. Only the commands and options used in the lessons are explained in this book. For comprehensive information about program features, refer to these resources:

• Adobe Audition Help, which you can view by choosing Help > Audition Help.

• Training and support resources on the Adobe Web site (www.adobe.com), which you can view by choosing Help > Adobe Online if you have a connection to the World Wide Web.

Adobe Certification

The Adobe Training and Certification Programs are designed to help Adobe customers improve and promote their product-proficiency skills. The Adobe Certified Expert (ACE) program is designed to recognize the high-level skills of expert users. Adobe Certified Training Providers (ACTP) use only Adobe Certified Experts to teach Adobe software classes. Available in either ACTP classrooms or on site, the ACE program is the best way to master Adobe products. For Adobe Certified Training Programs information, visit the Partnering with Adobe Web site at http://partners.adobe.com.

1 | A Quick Tour of Adobe Audition

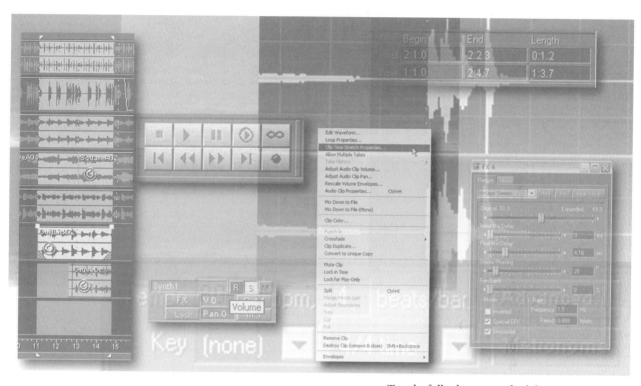

To take full advantage of Adobe Audition's extensive editing and conversion tools, it is important to understand how to navigate through a session, control audio playback, apply effects, and export files.

In this lesson, you will be introduced to the tools and interface used in Adobe Audition. Future lessons will provide more in-depth exercises and specific details as to how you can better take advantage of the tools. You'll start the tour by opening a partially completed session where you'll add the finishing touches to a 60 second jazz song. You will add music tracks, repair noisy audio, and then export the session to an mp3 audio file.

1   Start Adobe Audition, and click on the Multitrack View tab.

2   Choose File > Open Session, and open the 01_start.ses file in the AA_01 folder, which is located in the AA_CIB folder on your hard disk.

Note: If you have not already copied the resource files for this lesson onto your hard disk from the AA_01 folder from the Adobe Audition 1.5 Classroom in a Book *CD, do so now. See "Copying the Classroom in a Book files" on page 2.*

3   Choose File > Save Session As. Enter the name **01_Tour.ses**, and save the file in the AA_01 folder. This keeps the original file untouched, in case you want to return to the original source file.

4   To preview the finished session file, choose File > Open Session, and open the 01_end.ses file in the AA_01 folder. Play the completed session file by clicking on the Play from Cursor to End of View button (▶) in the Transport Controls toolbar, which is located in the lower left corner of the Audition window. You can also press the spacebar on your keyboard to play the session.

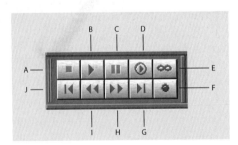

The Transport Controls. A. Stop. B. Play from Cursor to End of View. C. Pause.
D. Play from Cursor to End of File. E. Play Looped. F. Record. G. Go to End or Next Cue.
H. Fast Forward. I. Rewind. J. Go to Beginning or Previous Cue.

Note: You may need to maximize your window to see all controls available within Audition. When the window size is reduced, certain controls are not displayed. You can maximize your window by clicking the Maximize button in the upper right corner of the window.

5   When you are ready to start working, close the 01_end.ses file by choosing
File > Close Session and Its Media. If necessary, reopen the 01_Tour.ses file by choosing
File > Open Session and selecting the 01_Tour.ses.

Navigating the session

The 01_Tour.ses session is on your screen in Multitrack View. A list of the sound files
used in the session are listed along the left portion of the window in an area called the
Organizer window.

Adobe Audition work area. **A.** *Edit View tab* **B.** *Multitrack View tab* **C.** *CD Project tab* **D.** *Current-time Indicator.* **E.** *Toolbars.* **F.** *Display window.* **G.** *Various information windows.* **H.** *Current time* **I.** *Zoom tools.* **J.** *Transport Controls.* **K.** *Advanced Organizer window options.* **L.** *Organizer Window.*

The Multitrack View displays an audio clip on each track, and is located in the center of the screen. In the this session, each clip represents a musical instrument and each track has been labeled to identify the instrument used. You can navigate through a session using a number of different methods.

1   Press the Play button (▶) in the Transport Controls, which are located in the bottom left corner of the Audition window.

As the session begins to play, the playback cursor, which is displayed as a vertical white line, moves across the multitrack. Note the arrangement of the clips inside the multitrack. The first instrument is the UprightBass, which begins playing immediately. As the playback cursor hits the GruveDrm02 clip, you hear this component. The GrooveBass track represents another bass track. Each instrument is on a different track, yet the overall result is multiple instruments playing in synchronization.

2   Press the Pause button (⏸) to pause the session. The playback cursor stops and the current time is displayed at the bottom of the window. We paused our session at 15 seconds.

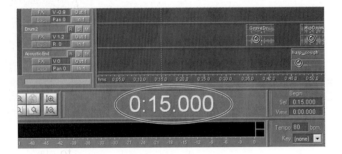

3   Click the Play button in the Transport Controls and note that the session begins at the start rather than resuming from the pause point. This is because the Play button always starts to play at the current-time indicator, which is represented by the yellow triangles located at the beginning of the session.

4   Press the spacebar on your keyboard to stop the playback. In addition to using the Transport controls, Audition offers many keyboard shortcuts to perform common commands. For example, you can use the spacebar to start or stop playback.

5   Place your cursor over one of the yellow current-time indicator triangles. Your cursor changes to a pointing finger (🖑), allowing you to move the current-time indicator to a specific point in the multitrack.

6   Click and drag the current-time indicator slowly across the multitrack to the 24 second mark. This position is also the beginning of the audio clip named SquareA01. The current-time indicator snaps to the beginning of the clip, unless the snapping options have been changed from Audition's default settings.

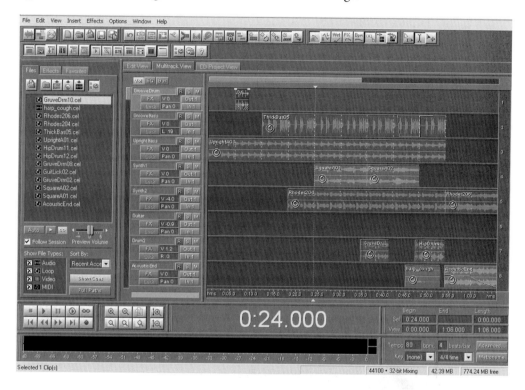

7   Click the Play button in the Transport controls, the session begins to play from the 24 second mark. The current-time indicator is used frequently to navigate and play specific sections within a session. Press the spacebar to stop playing the session.

8   Place your cursor over the ruler at the bottom of the multitrack, making sure the hand icon is displayed. Right-click on the ruler and a context menu is displayed. From the context menu choose the Display Time Format option. Select the Bars and Beats option and the ruler changes from the decimal format to Bars and Beats. This is a more traditional time display for working with loop-based files.

Note: *While this session was originally displaying time in a decimal format of hours, minutes, seconds, and milliseconds (HMS), you can change the units of measurement based upon your needs and the type of session you are creating.*

9   Click the Go to Beginning or Previous Cue button (⏮)in the Transport Controls to place the current-time indicator at the beginning of the session. At the start of the session the time display shows 1:1.00. This is read as 1 bar and 1 beat.

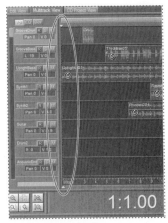

*The current-time indicator at the
beginning of the session.*

Working with loops

To better understand the concept of Bars and Beats, look in the Organizer window and notice, but don't select, the drum loop entitled GruveDrm02.cel. The .cel extension signifies that this file is an Audition file capable of being looped in the multitrack. This is the loop file used in the first track.

1   Press the spacebar to begin playing the session file. At the 3 bar 1 beat mark the GruveDrm02 clip plays for exactly one bar and then ends. When the drumbeat stops playing, press the spacebar to stop the playback cursor. In this session each bar consists of exactly four beats. Press the spacebar again and when the drum begins, count the four beats in the drum loop. When the bar is over, press the spacebar to stop playing the session.

2 Click once to select the GruveDrm02 clip in the Multitrack View. Place your cursor over the diagonal lines in the bottom right corner of the GruveDrm02 clip. Your cursor will change to a double arrow with a small loop icon ().

3 Click and drag the loop to the right, extending the loop so it ends at the same time as the clips in both track 2 and track 3, ThickBas05 and UprightA01 respectively. As you extend the loop, a dashed line is created with every new bar, helping you keep track of the number of bars, and ensuring that the clip ends precisely on a beat.

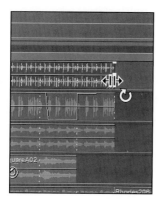

4 Press the Home key on your keyboard to place the current-time indicator at the beginning of the session, then press the spacebar to play the session. The drum track loops seamlessly for 16 bars. The original drum clip was one bar in length. You were able to extend the clip because the original file was designed to be looped. Press the spacebar to stop playback after you have reviewed the file.

Note: *Adobe Audition 1.5 ships with a Loopology CD of nearly 5,000 individual music loops sampled from a variety of musical sources. It is also possible to create your own loops in Audition's Edit View. You will explore this feature in Chapter 4.*

5   In the Organizer window, click on the Import File button (🖼) and select the file GuitLick02.cel in the AA_01 folder on your hard disk. Click Open to import the file into the Organizer window. Click and drag the file GuitLick02.cel into the empty track named Guitar. Place it near the beginning of the track and release the mouse.

Click and drag GuitLick02.cel to the empty Guitar track.

6   Select the Move/Copy Clip tool (➤✛) and then click on the GuitLick02 clip, drag it to the right in the Multitrack View.

The Move/Copy tool is in the tool section.

As you drag the clip into the multitrack, notice that the beginning and the end of the clip snap to the individual beats on the ruler. Drag the clip so the beginning aligns with the 11 bar mark. A vertical white line appears when the clip is aligned to this position. Make sure the white line is aligning at the beginning of the clip, not the end.

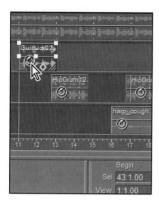

Note: It is useful to refer to the status bar at the bottom of the window. As you move clips through the multitrack, the status bar reflects the location of the start of the clip.

7 Place your cursor on the handle at the end of the GuitLick02 clip. Extend the clip two bars to the 15 bar 1 beat mark by clicking and dragging the diagonal handle to the right.

8 Click and drag the current-time indicator to the 8 bar 1 beat mark (8:1.00) and then press the spacebar on your keyboard to play the session from this point.

Muting and soloing tracks

Audition provides tools to make it easier to work with multiple tracks.

1 Click and drag the current-time indicator to the 9 bar mark (9:1.00). This is the point that the clip SquareA01 in the Synth1 track begins. To make it easier to separate a single instrument from the others, you can listen to just a single track using Audition's solo and mute options.

2 Press the spacebar on your keyboard to play the session. In the Synth1 track click the yellow S button (⬛). All other tracks except the Synth are temporarily turned off. The other clips become grayed-out to visually identify that they are not audible. Press the spacebar to stop the playback cursor. Click the Solo button again to make the other tracks audible.

3 In the Synth1 track, click the M button (⬛).The SquareA01 clip becomes grayed-out, indicating that it will not be audible. Press the spacebar to begin playing the session, after a few seconds click the M button and the SquareA01 clip becomes audible. Both the Mute and Solo buttons work in real time as a session is playing. Press the spacebar to stop playing the session.

4 Click and drag the current-time indicator to the 7 bar 1 beat mark. Click the Solo button for the GrooveDrum track. Hold down the Ctrl key and also click on the Solo button for the Synth2 track. Press the spacebar to play the Drum track and the Synth2 tracks only. Ctrl-clicking the Solo button on two or more tracks allows you to play only those tracks together.

5 Press the spacebar to stop playing the session. Ctrl-click on the Solo buttons for the GrooveDrum track and the Synth2 track to enable the remaining tracks.

Changing track volume and pan

You can modify the Volume and Pan properties of each track in a multitrack session. All clips located within the track are affected by these changes.

1   Click on the Solo button in the Synth1 track to isolate the Synth track. Click and drag the current-time indicator to the 9 bar 1 beat mark. Press the spacebar to begin playing the session. In the Synth1 track properties, place your cursor in the text box marked V 0. This is the volume control for this track, measured in decibels.

2   With your cursor still in the volume control for the Synth1 track, click and drag your cursor to the right, raising the volume of the Synth1 track to 10 dB. You will immediately hear this change. Click and drag the volume control to the left, continuing past 0 to -7 dB. As you change the values to a negative number, the volume is lower than the original setting. Click and drag back to the right to return the value to 0. Click on the Solo button to enable the remaining tracks.

3   If necessary, press the spacebar to stop playing the session. Press the Home key to return the current-time indicator to the beginning of the multitrack, and then press the spacebar again to play the session from the beginning.

4   In the UprightBass track, place your cursor in the text box marked Pan 0. Click and drag to the left to change the percentage of the left channel to L 75. Note the change in real time as the Bass plays primarily in the left channel. Click and drag to the right to change the value to R 30.

Note: Depending on the speaker setup of your computer system, changes to Pan levels may be more apparent when listening to the audio using headphones. The stereo speakers on a laptop or the built-in speakers of a computer may not provide sufficient distance between left and right channels to make pan effects immediately noticeable.

5   Press the spacebar to stop playback of the session.

Changing volume using Track Envelopes

Track Envelopes allow you to change the levels for volume, pan and other audio effects over the time of the clip. For example, you may wish to dynamically change the volume levels to fade an instrument out at the end of a clip, or you may wish to create a stereo effect of a sound panning from left to right.

1 Click on the ThickBass05 clip in the GrooveBass track to select it. Click the Solo button to turn off all the other tracks. At the top of your screen, click the Show Volume Envelopes button (📓) if it is not already selected. Volume Envelopes appear on all the audio clips in the track when this button is depressed. Volume Envelopes are located at the top of a clip by default. You can see the change in the envelopes in this track at the 15 bar mark.

2 Click on the Edit Envelopes button (📓) if it is not already selected to view the anchor points located on the volume envelope. Click and drag the current-time indicator to the 14 bar mark (14:1.00) and press the spacebar on your keyboard. When the playback cursor reaches the 15 bar mark, the bass track is inaudible, but one bar later in the clip the volume returns and the track is audible. The anchor points located at the top of a clip represent 100% volume. Anchor points located at the bottom of a clip represent 0% volume, which is silence. You can use this feature to create a fade-out effect.

3 Click the Solo button in the Synth2 track, then click the last clip in this track, Rhodes206, so it is selected. Move the current-time indicator to the 21 bar mark (21:1.00).

4 Using the current-time indicator as a guide, place your cursor on the volume envelope at the top of the clip. Your cursor will change to a hand with a plus sign. Click and release on the volume envelope to add an anchor point. Move your cursor to the far right side of the clip. Click and drag the last anchor point at the end of the clip all the way to the bottom. The volume indicator next to your cursor changes as you move your cursor, when the cursor reaches the bottom it reads Vol 0%.

5   Press the spacebar to play the clip to the end of the track. The organ clip fades out to silence.

6   Hold down the Ctrl key and click on the first anchor point in the Rhodes206 clip and drag down to approximately 85%. The first two anchor points now move in unison, doing so reduces the overall volume of the clip.

Ctrl-clicking any anchor point will allow you to move all anchor points up or down in order to increase or decrease overall volume. Continue to depress the Ctrl key while moving the anchor points.

7   Click the Solo button on the GrooveBass track to enable the audio for the other tracks.

Adding non-destructive effects

Audition allows you to apply various audio effects such as Echo or Reverb to individual clips. These effects are non-destructive, as they do not alter the original sound file in any way.

1   Click the Solo button on the Guitar track to mute the other tracks.

2   Click the Time Selection tool (🔳) located at the top right side of the window. Click and drag over the length of the entire GuitLick02 clip to select this clip. Press the spacebar to preview this clip before you add an effect to it.

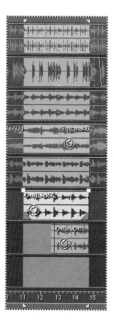

3   Click on the FX button (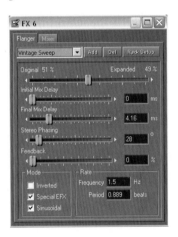) located next to the volume control in the Guitar track properties. The Track 6 Effects Rack window opens.

Note: It may be necessary to expand the size of the Track Properties portion of the window to see this button. If this button is not visible, click and drag, to the right, the line separating the Track Properties from the Multitrack display. After clicking the FX button, you may need to move the window to see both the GuitLick02 clip in the multitrack and the Effects Rack window at the same time.

4   Click on the plus sign (⊞) next to the Delay Effects category and select Flanger. Click the Add button to add this to the Current Effects Rack. Click the OK button to add the default Flanger effect, which adds a varying, short delay to the Guitar clip.

5   Click on the FX 6 button again and the FX 6 window appears with the Flanger controls. In the FX 6 window, click the drop-down menu and select the Vintage Sweep preset.

6   Click on the Mixer tab at the top of the FX 6 window to view the Mixing controls. The first mixer named Dry Out is used to control the percentage of the original guitar signal. This value is currently 0. The second mixer named Flanger controls the percentage of the Flanger effect, this value is currently 100.

7   Press the spacebar to play the guitar selection and hear the Flanger effect. If necessary, press the spacebar to repeat playback as you make adjustments in the next steps.

8   In the Flanger mixer, click the Bypass button (Bypass) to hear the original signal. Click the Bypass button again and drag the Flanger slider down to 80, now drag the Dry Out slider up to 20. This moderately decreases the Flanger effect and also returns a small percentage of the original guitar signal back into the mix.

9   Click the Close button in the upper right corner to close the FX window.

10   Click the Solo button in the Guitar track to turn on the other tracks and to hear the results of the Flanger effect as applied to the Guitar. Press the spacebar to stop playing the session.

Using hiss reduction

Working non-destructively with envelopes and effects is a very powerful way to perform edits. Audition also performs destructive edits that change the original source files when you work using the Edit View. There are features of Audition which are only available in the Edit View, such as Noise and Hiss Reduction along with the Spectral View.

1   In the Multitrack View display window, in the track named Acoustic End, double-click on the clip harp_cough.cel to enter the Edit View. The entire audio file is displayed as an audio waveform.

Note: While in Edit View there are certain commands available that are not in the Multitrack. You can always switch between views by clicking on the Edit View or Multitrack View tabs located near the top of the window.

2   Press the Home key on your keyboard to place the current-time indicator at the beginning of the file and then press the spacebar to play the file from beginning to end. The source for this file was a live performance. The original recording includes a slight hiss along with a cough at the end of the harp, which impacts the final file. You will remove these deficiencies in the file using tools available in the Edit View.

3   Choose Edit > Select Entire Wave to select the entire harp_cough clip.

4   Choose Effects > Noise Reduction > Hiss Reduction to open the Hiss Reduction window.

5   In the Hiss Reduction window, select Standard Hiss Reduction from the list of presets, and then click Preview. The hiss decreases dramatically after applying this effect. To hear the difference, select the bypass option and the hiss returns. Click the OK button to commit the change.

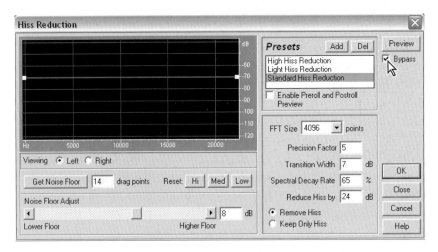

6   Press the spacebar to play the modified file. Although the hiss has been reduced, the cough still remains.

7   Click the Multitrack View tab and press the Home key to place the current-time indicator at the beginning of the session.Then move the current-time indicator to the 15 bar mark (15:1.0). Press the spacebar to play the session. The hiss is reduced when previewing the file in the session because changes made to a file in Edit View are automatically updated to the file in the Multitrack.

Using the Spectral View

One of the unique features of Adobe Audition is its ability to display and edit sound files in the Spectral View.

1 Double-click on the Harp_cough.cel clip in the Acoustic End track to display the waveform in the Edit View.

2 Choose View > Spectral View to display the waveform. The x-axis, which is shown horizontally, is displaying the total time of the loop. The y-axis, which is shown vertically, is measuring the frequency.

Note: If an alert message is displayed regarding new selection tools, click OK to close the alert window.

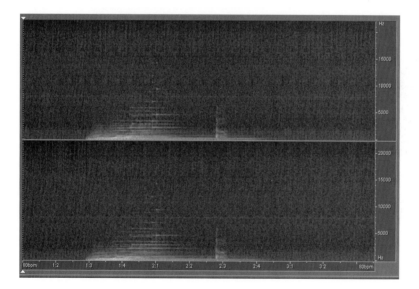

3 Press the Home key on your keyboard to place the current-time indicator at the beginning of the clip and then press the spacebar to play the file. The greater a sound's amplitude within a certain frequency, the brighter the colors. For example, it is very easy to note the cough at the end of the file.

4   Choose the Marquee Selection tool (▦) from the tools and buttons located at the top of the window. Click and drag a marquee selection around the entire spectral representation of the cough. Press the spacebar to play only the selection. Listen carefully and you can also hear the diminishing tone of the harp. Be careful to not select too large of an area beyond the cough.

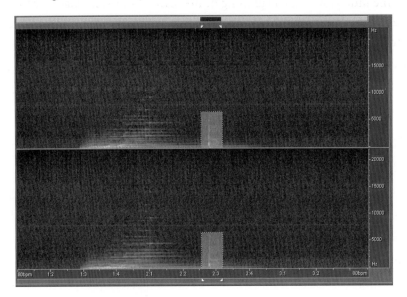

5   Choose Effects > Noise Reduction > Click/Pop Eliminator to open the Click/Pop Eliminator. This effect is applied only to the selection you made with the Marquee tool.

Note: If the selected area is too large, this option is not available.

6   Click the Fill Single Click Now button at the bottom of the Click/Pop Eliminator window. Audition processes the file and applies the effect.

7   Press the spacebar again and the selection loops. The cough has been removed, yet the diminishing tones of the harp have been preserved.

8   Press the Home key to place the current-time indicator at the beginning of the clip. Press the Play button or the spacebar to hear the edited version of the harp file.

Changing the tempo of an entire session

Once you have created a final version of a song you have the flexibility in Audition to change the tempo, in other words, to make a session faster or slower.

1   Click on the Multitrack View to return to the session, press the Home key to return the current-time indicator to the beginning of the session. Press the spacebar to begin playing. Listen to the session for three or four bars to get a sense of the tempo and then press the spacebar to stop playing.

2   In the Session Properties window in the lower right hand corner, click to place your cursor in the text box marked Tempo 80 bpm—bpm represents beats per minute and determines the rhythmic speed of the song.

3   Double-click in the text box to highlight the number 80 and enter **100**. Press the Enter key and Audition will update the session, which may take a few moments. All the tracks are time-stretched to match the session's tempo.

4   Press the Home key on your keyboard to place the current-time indicator at the beginning of your session. Press the spacebar to play. The updated session has a faster tempo of 100 beats per minute, yet the original pitch of the instruments has not changed.

You can always type in a new number to update the tempo of session. However if you want to compare tempos, you can use the shortcut Ctrl + Z to undo the tempo change and return to the original tempo for that purpose.

Exporting a session to mp3 audio format

Audition can export audio files in many different file formats, including the mp3 format.

1   Choose File > Save Session As. Navigate to your AA_01 folder and enter the name **01final.ses**.

2   Choose File > Export > Audio. If this is your first time exporting audio, an Edit Original Options window opens. Click Yes to close this window and then in the Save as Type menu choose mp3Pro.

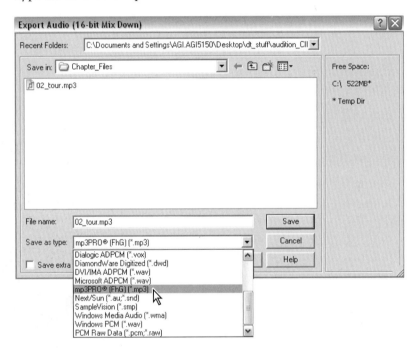

3   Click the Options button and the mp3 Encoder window opens.

4   In the mp3 Encoder window, click the preset menu in the upper left corner and select 192 kbps Stereo, then click OK. Click Save to export the mp3. The mp3 file is saved to your hard drive and can be opened in Audition or using any hardware or software capable of playing mp3 audio files.

5   Choose File > Close All.

Congratulations! You have completed the lesson.

2 Audition Basics

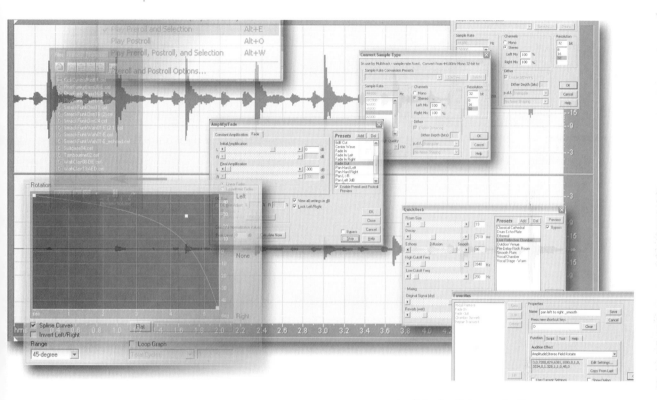

Audition's editing tools allow you to quickly and easily manipulate audio clips. You can select portions of audio clips for editing, and preview files before placing them into a session. Take advantage of Audition's customizable working environment and use three separate views to efficiently navigate through sessions and files.

In this lesson, you'll learn how to do the following:

• Use the Multitrack and Edit Views.

• Work with the Selection/View controls.

• Learn to use the Transport controls.

• Learn to use the Zoom controls.

• Use Windows in Audition.

Getting started

Adobe Audition displays your work using three views: the Multitrack View, the Edit View, and the CD Project View. This lesson is focused on the common features among the three views. Each view is also discussed specifically in Lessons 3, 4 and 12. When you open Audition sessions, the Multitrack View is displayed. Adobe Audition sessions are project files which, in turn, point to sound or music files.

1   Start Adobe Audition, and select the Multitrack View tab.

Note: If you have not already copied the resource files for this lesson onto your hard disk from the AA_02 folder from the Adobe Audition 1.5 Classroom in a Book *CD, do so now. See "Copying the Classroom in a Book files" on page 2.*

2   To review the finished session file, choose File > Open Session. Navigate to the AA_ CIB folder you copied to your hard disk, and open the file "02_end.ses" in the AA_02 folder. Click the Play from Cursor to End of File button (▣) in the Transport Controls. The completed file is played for you.

The Play to End button on the Transport Controls.

3   Close the 02_end.ses file by choosing File > Close Session and Its Media.

4   Choose File > Open Session, and open the 02_start.ses file in the AA_02 folder, which is located in the AA_CIB folder on your hard disk.

When you open an existing session in Audition, the program will take a few moments to load the existing sound files into the session window. At the bottom of the application window is a status bar, displaying useful information about the session.

Place your cursor over the various clips in the multitrack session. The names of the loops used in the session are displayed in the status bar. The sample rate is 44,100 Hz, which is Audition's default sample rate, as well the sample rate for compact discs, and the size of the complete file is approximately 145 megabytes. The last number displays the amount of free space available for storage in your hard drive. While this is the default layout for the status bar, right-clicking on status bar lets you add or remove information about the session, therefore your status bar can look different.

*A. Clip name. **B.** Sample rate. **C.** Size of file. **D.** Free space on your hard drive.*

Audition session files

It is important to remember that Adobe Audition's session files, which are identified by their .ses file extension, contain no audio data. Each session file points to other audio files on your computer or network. The Audition session file keeps track of where the audio files are stored on your computer, each file's duration and location within the session, along with the envelopes and effects that are applied to the tracks.

A session file is dependent upon the audio files to which it points, so it's important to keep your files organized. As you are getting started with Audition, it is a good idea to keep all files related to a session in the same folder. Adobe Audition provides an option to save a copy of all files used in a session, including the session file, into the same folder.

About sample rates

During the sampling process, an incoming analog signal is sampled at discrete time intervals. Each interval of analog signal is momentarily observed, and thus, each represents a specific, measurable voltage level. A mathematical conversion generates a digital series of numbers that represent the signal level at that particular point in time. The generated data can be digitally stored or processed.

*The **sample rate** is the number of samples (or snapshots) that are taken of an audio signal per second. For example, a sample rate of 44,100 Hz means that 44,100 samples are taken per second. Since sampling is tied directly to the component of time, a system's sample rate determines a system's overall bandwidth—in other words, how many frequencies can be encoded within the audio signal. Higher sample rates generally yield a better quality waveform.*

The most common sample rates for digital audio editing are as follows:
- *11,025 Hz—Poor AM Radio Quality/Speech (low-end multimedia)*
- *22,050 Hz—Near FM Radio Quality (high-end multimedia)*
- *32,000 Hz—Better than FM Radio Quality (standard broadcast rate)*
- *44,100 Hz—CD Quality*
- *48,000 Hz—DAT Quality*
- *96,000 Hz—DVD Quality*

—From Adobe Audition Help

5   To view the entire session from beginning to end, click the Zoom Out Full Both Axis tool () located in the Zoom controls, along the bottom of the window. This is a convenient way to view all the tracks in your session. If your Selection/View Controls window is not currently open, choose Window > Selection/View Controls. This window displays the entire length of your current view and the view should read approximately 1:22:708.

6   Choose View > Display Time Format > Bars and Beats. The units in the timeline ruler at the bottom of the screen are now bars and beats as are the units in the selection/view controls. The length of your session in bars and beats should be 32:2.15. Audition can be used for a different types of projects. Different projects require different time displays. This session opened with a time display of hours, minutes, seconds, and milliseconds and you changed it to bars and beats. Working with loops is often easier with a time display of Bars and Beats.

7   Choose the Move/Copy Clip tool (✛) and click the last clip in Track 1, which is the drum track. Drag the clip to the right to move it, then choose Ctrl+Z to undo the move thereby returning the clip to its original position. This tool allows you to change the location of clips in a session. If an alert message appears informing you of new tools, click OK to close the window.

Note: There are three tools in Audition for moving and selecting clips. The Move/Copy Clip tool (✛), the Time Selection tool (I), and the Hybrid tool (▣).

8   Click the Time Selection tool (I) and place your cursor approximately halfway into the SmackFunkDrm18 clip, which is the first clip located in the first track. Click and drag to the left, selecting the first half of the clip. Notice the selection covers all 5 tracks of the session, not just the first track. Adobe Audition's Multitrack View allows you to add audio files to different tracks of a session in order to create a multi-layered sound composition. For example, while playing a session, you can adjust the volume of any track in real time. Final sessions are then mixed down for use in a CD or as a sound file such as a WAV or mp3. In Lesson 4 you will be exploring the mixing capabilities in the Multitrack View.

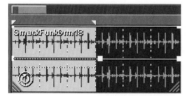

Note: The Hybrid tool combines the functionality of both the Move/Copy Clip tool and the Time Selection tool. When using this tool, the left-click on a two-button mouse functions as the Time Selection tool, while the right-click functions as the Move/Copy Clip tool.

9   Click the Zoom to Selection tool (⊞). Click the Play button (▶) and only the view within the display window is played. When the playback cursor reaches the end of the display window, it stops. Use this method to preview certain sections of your tracks.

10   Click the Play from Cursor to End of File button (◉) and the entire session plays. When the playback cursor reaches the end of the display window, it will continue playing until it reaches the end of the session.

11   Click the Stop button at any point.

12   Place your cursor over the green horizontal scroll bar, directly above track 1. You will see the Hand icon (✋) appear, click and drag to the right or left, scrolling through the session.

13   Place your cursor on the right edge of the green horizontal scroll bar. The cursor changes to a magnifying glass with arrows. Click and drag to the right to zoom out horizontally. Click and drag to the left to zoom in horizontally. Do this three times to get a sense of how this tool works.

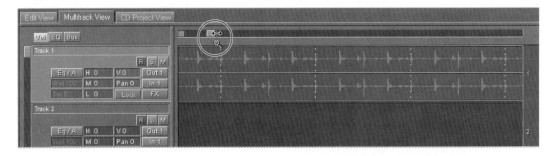

14   Click the Zoom Out Vertically button (⊟) to expand the view and see all the tracks in the session. While Audition can use up to 128 audio tracks per session, the number of concurrently visible tracks is dependent upon the display resolution of your monitor. Being able to change your view allows you to see more tracks or to focus on a portion of a specific track. Click the Zoom Out Full Both Axis button (⊞) to restore the initial view.

15   Click to select the Hybrid tool (⊡). Left-click at the start of the multitrack session and drag to the right, selecting the first eight bars of the session. Press the Play button to play these eight bars.

16 Click the right range marker, which is the yellow button at the top and bottom of the selection range, and drag it to 11 bars 1 beat. Then click and drag the left range marker, which is also yellow, to the 7 bars 1 beat position. All 4 bars in this region are selected. Press the play button to play the selection.

If necessary, use the Selection/View controls, located in the bottom right corner of the window, to help you make the selection. These were discussed in step 5 of this exercise.

You can expand or reduce the range of your selection by moving either of the yellow range markers to the left or the right.

Using the Organizer Window

The loops used in the current session are listed in the Organizer window. By default, Audition lists the current samples in the order in which they were imported or accessed, with the most recently imported file at the top.

1 Change your sort order from Recent Access to Filename by clicking on the Sort By: menu at the bottom of the Organizer window. This places your files in alphabetical order.

Note: If you do not see the Advanced Organizer window options, press the Advanced Options button (⬚) in the upper right of the Organizer window.

2 The first two files are Kick&Sizzle.cel and KickCymbalRoll01.cel. Notice the Audio icon (⬚) next to the file names. This marks files as Audio file types.

3 If not already selected, select the Play Looped button () at the bottom of the Organizer Window and then select the PhatFunkyBass08-E.cel loop by clicking on it once, then press the Play button (▶) at the bottom of the Organizer window. The sound loops continuously from beginning to end until you press the Stop button (■). Notice that these buttons are in the Organizer window, not the Transport Controls.

Note: If you accidentally double-click on the files in the Organizer window, they open in the Edit View for editing. Return to the Multitrack View by clicking the Multitrack tab across the top of the window or choose View > Multitrack.

4 Click the AutoPlay button (Auto) at the bottom of the Organizer window, and then click on each file to automatically play it. You do not have to wait for a file to end before previewing the next file. Use the Down Arrow key on your keyboard to navigate through your list of files one at a time. You can also adjust the Preview Volume slider to raise or lower the volume of the files. Press the Stop button when you are done previewing the files.

Working with toolbars and windows

Much of your work in Audition will involve switching between the Edit View and the Multitrack View.

1 Click on the Edit Waveform View button ( ) in the View Toggle toolbar.

Your workspace changes from the Multitrack View to the Edit View. The Edit View is used to modify a single audio waveform, examples might include adding an effect or deleting part of a clip. Changes made to files in the Edit View are destructive: adding an effect or trimming a loop will change the original file once it is saved. Edits made in the Multitrack View are non-destructive, meaning the original file remains untouched.

2 Click on the Multitrack View button (▦) to return to the Multitrack.

3 Click on the CD Project View button (◎) to display this screen. The Organizer window stays consistent between the three views, however the menu commands are different in each of the views.

4 Click on the Multitrack View tab. You can also use the Edit View, Multitrack View, and CD Project View tabs to switch between these three views.

5 Double-click on the first clip in Track 1, SmackFunkDrm18.cel, to enter the Edit View. The selected clip automatically displays its waveform. Click on the Multitrack View tab to return to Multitrack View.

6 Double-click the loop file Suitcase04.cel in the Organizer window. This is another method to enter the Edit View. Return to the Multitrack View by pressing the number 9 on your keyboard.

♀ *Audition uses a variety of keyboard commands including numbers, letters and function keys. You can customize keyboard shortcuts by choosing Options > Keyboard Shortcuts and Midi Triggers and assigning or modifying keys to access specific commands or effects.*

7 From the menu choose View > Toolbars > Window Toggles. Toolbars which are currently open have a checkmark beside them. If Window Toggles does not have a checkmark select it now, this adds the Window Toggles toolbar to your main window.

8 Right-click anywhere on the Window Toggles toolbar, which you selected in the last step. Right-clicking on any toolbar reveals a context menu with a list of all the toolbars. As with the list displayed under the View menu, toolbars with a checkmark beside them are currently open, unchecked toolbars are hidden. Select the Window Toggles option to remove the toolbar.

♀ *You can right-click on any toolbar to access its context menu, and then select Window Toggles to display the toolbar.*

9   Place your cursor over the first button in the toolbar. A Tool tip appears describing the function of the button. Tool tips also display the keyboard shortcut in brackets.

10   Click the Hide/Show Mixer button () in the toolbar to display the Mixers window. You will use the Mixers window to control the master volume of the entire session. The Mixers window also provides controls for each track.

11   Click the Mixers window along the top of the title bar. Drag the window to the right side of the main window. While dragging the window, move your cursor to the right edge of the window. When the right edge of the window becomes highlighted, release the mouse. The mixer window attaches to the main window.

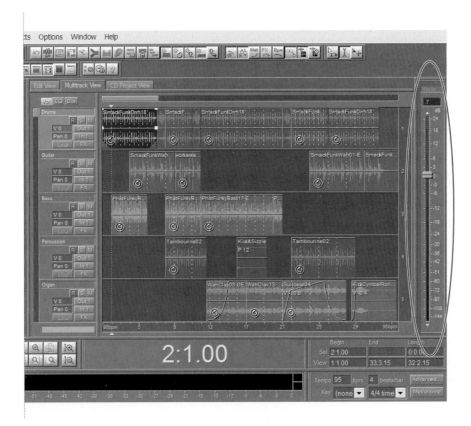

Placing individual windows into areas of the main interface is referred to as docking. Docking the mixer window allows you to control the volume of your multitrack session in real time. In general, docking windows is preferable to displaying a window which may interfere with the view of your tracks and track controls.

12 Place your cursor over the vertical double bars on the left side of the Zoom Controls until the cursor changes (⊞). Click and drag the window up to remove it from the dock. Practice docking windows by dragging the Zoom Controls window back to its original location. You can dock or float most of Audition's windows, which is especially useful if you work with multiple monitors attached to your computer.

13 Using the Hybrid tool (⊞) in the upper right of the toolbar, click and drag in Track 5, making a selection starting at 8 bars 1 beat and ending at the 12 bars 1 beat mark. You may have to adjust the range boundaries, represented by the yellow triangles at the corner of the selected area, to make the selection. Use your Selection/View window in the bottom right corner to confirm the length of the selection. You should have a total selection of 4 bars.

14 Click the Play Looped button () in the Transform controls. This loops the selection continuously, until you click the Stop button. Playing a looped selection is a useful way to preview changes to your session in real time. As the session is playing, move the slider in the mixer window toward the top to increase the overall volume and toward the bottom to decrease it. Keep an eye on your Level Meter window at the bottom and notice how it changes as you move the slider. Press the spacebar to stop playing the session.

15 In the number field at the top of the Mixer window, which you docked earlier in this exercise, highlight the current value and enter **0**. The levels return to their default value of zero.

Level Meters

The Level Meters represent the incoming signal in dBFS (decibels below full scale), where a level of 0 dB is the maximum amplitude possible before clipping (also known as distortion) occurs. Yellow peak indicators remain for 1.5 seconds to allow for reading of the peak amplitude. If clipping does occur, the clip indicator to the right of the meter lights up and stays on until you clear it. When stereo audio is displayed, the top meter represents the left channel, and the bottom represents the right.

You can customize the Level Meters in a variety of ways, such as changing the decibel range, showing valley (minimum amplitude) indicators, and changing the mode of the peak indicators.

—From Adobe Audition Help

Note: *As you begin to add more tracks to a session, you will generally need to lower your master mixer volume to prevent clipping. If your clip indicators are red, click on them to clear them.*

Customizing the Multitrack View

Audition is capable of handling up to 128 audio tracks per session. There are five tracks of sound loops in this session.

1 To make sure you are seeing all the tracks in your session, click the Zoom Out Full Both Axis tool ().

2   In the track controls for Track 1, click once on the name Track 1 and enter **Drums** in the name text box. In the track controls for track 2, enter **Guitar** in the name text box. Repeat these steps for tracks 3, 4 and 5, entering **Bass**, **Percussion** and **Organ** respectively. It is useful to rename your tracks based on their content.

3   Change the color of the first "SmackFunkDRm18" clip in the drum track by right-clicking it and choosing Clip Color from the context menu. In the Clip Color window, choose the first red shade in the upper left and click OK. Modifying the color of individual sound clips in Audition is useful for visually identifying different instruments or loops. We have color-coded the session for you but have left the first clip as the default green.

4   Choose File > Save Session to update the 02.start.ses file.

5   Choose File > Close All.

Review questions

1   What is the difference between the Edit View and Multitrack View?

2   What is the quickest way to view all the tracks from beginning to end in your Multitrack View?

3   Where are the Move/Copy Clip tool, the Time Selection tool, and the Hybrid tool located, and how are these tools different?

Review answers

1   Edit View uses a destructive method, which permanently alters a sound wave when the file is saved. Permanent changes are preferable when converting sample rate and bit depth, mastering, or batch processing. Multitrack View uses a nondestructive method, which is not permanent, but requires more processing power. The flexibility of the Multitrack View is preferable when working with multi-layered musical compositions or video soundtracks.

2   The Zoom Out Full Both Axis tool (🔍) automatically scales your timeline to show every track in your session, as well as the entire clip within each track.

3   The Move/Copy Clip tool, the Time Selection tool and the Hybrid tool are all located in the Multitrack Tools toolbar and can be accessed by View > Toolbars > Multitrack Tools. Left-clicking with the Move/Copy Clip tool moves a clip from one area of the multitrack to another, Right-clicking reveals a menu allowing you to create a copy of the clip. Left-clicking with the Time Selection tool selects a portion or all of a waveform, right-clicking does nothing. Left-clicking with the Hybrid tool makes a selection for editing, while right-clicking moves a clip from one area of the multitrack to another.

On your own

1   Become more familiar with Audition's extended right-click functionality. Right-click on a clip and access the Adjust Audio Clip Volume window from the context menu. Right-click on an empty portion of a track and choose Track Volume. Right-click on the track and experiment with using the Mute and Solo commands from the context menu, rather than the multitrack controls.

2   Grab the Mixer window, which you docked in step 11 in the Working with Toolbars and Windows section. (If the Mixer window is not currently open, choose Window > Mixer.) Practice docking the Mixer window into different sections of the interface.

3   Use the Time Selection tool to make a selection in your multitrack session. Use the Zoom to Selection tool, the Zoom In to Left Edge of Selection tool and the Zoom In to Right Edge of Selection tool to view the results of each tool.

4   Audition also makes use of a mouse with a scroll wheel. Try the following: Place your cursor over the Horizontal Portion bar and scroll down to zoom out. Place your cursor over the time display and scroll up to zoom in. Place your cursor over a track name and scroll up and down to zoom out vertically.

3 | Working in the Edit View

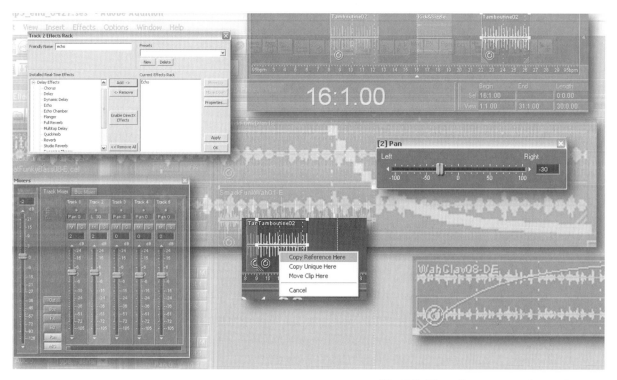

The Edit View allows you to view and edit audio files in a waveform display. Editing is simple with Audition's selection tools, allowing you to cut, copy, mix and trim audio clips with precision. Effects such as Normalization and Stereo Field Rotate can easily be applied and also saved as favorites. The Preroll and Postroll Preview makes working with effects easier than ever.

In this lesson, you'll learn how to do the following:

• Select and edit waveforms.

• Save a selection as a new file.

• Normalize a waveform.

• Apply effects and save as favorites.

• Add a filter.

Getting started

In this lesson, you'll work with a series of files in the Edit View.

1 Start Adobe Audition. Click on the Multitrack View tab if it is not already selected.

2 Choose File > Open Session, and open the 03_start.ses file located in the AA_03 folder, in the AA_CIB folder on your hard disk.

Note: If you have not already copied the resource files for this lesson onto your hard disk from the AA_03 folder from the Adobe Audition 1.5 Classroom in a Book *CD, do so now. See "Copying the Classroom in a Book files" on page 2.*

3 Choose File > Save Session As, and name the file **03_EditView.ses**, and save it in the AA_03 folder on your hard disk.

This Audition file is the same one you navigated in Lesson 2. In this lesson, you will be working with this file primarily in the Edit View.

4 To review the finished session file for this lesson, choose File > Open Session, and open the 03_end.ses file in the AA_03 folder, which is located within the AA_CIB folder on your hard disk. Press the Home key on your keyboard and then play the session file by either clicking on the Play button (▶) in the Transport Controls toolbar or pressing the spacebar on your keyboard.

5 When you are ready to start working, you can close the 03_end.ses file by choosing File > Close Session and Its Media. Then, choose File > Open Session to re-open the 03_EditView.ses file.

Using the Edit View

By default your session opens in the Multitrack View. To change to the Edit View, click on the Edit View tab or press the Edit Waveform View button (). The loops used in the session are displayed in the Organizer window along the left side of the display. They are listed according to the Sort By field in the bottom of the Organizer window.

You can also use the keyboard shortcut F12 to switch between the Edit View and the Multitrack View when either of these views is the active window.

1   If it is currently highlighted, click on the Loop button (∞) at the bottom of the Organizer window to deselect it. Click the PhatFunkyBass08-E.cel file in the Organizer window and then click the Play button. The clip plays once from beginning to end.

2   Click on the Loop button (∞) at the bottom of the Organizer window to highlight it, and then click the Play button. The sound plays repeatedly until you click the Stop button (■).

3   Double-click on the file Tambourine02.cel in the Organizer window to view its waveform. Click the Play button (▶) in the Transport Controls (not the Play button in the Organizer window). Note the peaks of the visual waveform, which represent the loudest sections of the loop, additional there is only a single waveform because this is a mono file. To play the tambourine sample in a loop, click the Play Looped button (∞) in the Transport Controls. Wait until it loops once and then press the spacebar to stop playing the file.

4   Double-click on the loop KickCymbalRoll01.cel. Two waveforms are displayed in this file because it is a stereo file. The waveform for the left channel appears at the top and the waveform for the right channel appears at the bottom. Place your cursor on the white line just above the top waveform display. When the letter "L" appears, click to isolate the left channel of the loop, the bottom waveform is grayed out, indicating that it is not audible. Press the spacebar to listen to the left channel only. Depending on the audio setup of your computer, the stereo effect may be more noticeable with a pair of headphones. If you hear the audio in the right channel and not the left, be sure your speakers or headphones are properly oriented.

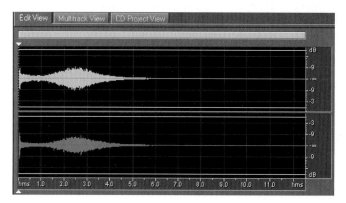

Note: Clicking on the white line at the bottom of the display will isolate the right channel only. Click in the middle of the display to restore the clip to its default stereo state.

Sound waves

Sound is created by vibrations, such as those produced by a guitar string, vocal cords, or a speaker cone. These vibrations move the air molecules near them, forcing molecules together, and as a result raising the air pressure slightly. The air molecules that are under pressure then push on the air molecules surrounding them, which push on the next set of air molecules, and so forth, causing a wave of high pressure to move through the air; as high pressure waves move through the air, they leave low pressure areas behind them. When these pressure lows and highs—or waves—reach us, they vibrate the receptors in our ears, and we hear the vibrations as sound. When you see a visual waveform that represents audio, that waveform represents these pressure waves. The zero line in the waveform is the pressure of air at rest. When the line swings up, it represents higher pressure, and when it swings low, it represents lower pressure. This waveform is the equivalent of the pressure waves in the air.

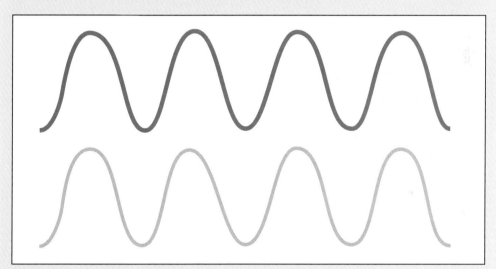

Sound waves represented as visual waveforms.

—From Adobe Audition Help

Selecting and editing waveforms

You may need to isolate a section of a waveform to apply an effect, listen to a section of sound more carefully, or trim an unwanted section of the sound. In this section you will select and edit a section of a waveform.

1   Double-click in an empty area of the Organizer window (below the file list) to import a new file into the Edit View.

*Double-click in an empty area
to import a new file.*

2   When the Import window appears, navigate to the AA_03 folder on your hard disk and select the ZildjianSizzle.cel file, and then click Open. The file is imported into your Organizer window.

3   Choose File Name from the Sort By drop-down menu in the Organizer window. The ZildjianSizzle.cel file appears at the bottom of your file list. Double-click this file to display the waveform. The name of the waveform is displayed at the top of your Audition window. Press the spacebar to play the file.

4 Choose Edit > Copy to New to make a new copy of this sound loop. When you are working in the Edit View, all changes you make to a sound file are destructive. Making a copy of your file ensures that your original sound file remains untouched. You can close the original ZildjianSizzle.cel file by right-clicking the file name in the Organizer window and choosing Close Files in the context menu.

5 The copied file is named ZildjianSizzle (2)*. The asterisk at the end of the filename indicates that this file is unsaved. This is a useful indicator for files that you are working on but have not saved. Save this copy now by choosing File > Save As from the file menu. When the Save As window appears, name this file **ZildjianSizzle_edited.cel** and click the Save button.

Note: You may receive a warning message regarding saving files to a compressed file format. The .cel files which are the native file format for Audition loops are similar to mp3 files in that audio data is compressed in order to reduce file size. However, the default compression rate for cel files is 320 Kbps, which is extremely high and causes next to no detectable loss of quality. Click OK to close the alert window, if necessary.

6 Double-click the ZildjianSizzle_edited file to view its waveform. This audio file has a few seconds of silence at the end of the sample which you will remove. If your time display is not in Decimal format (hours, minutes, seconds, milliseconds), change it now by choosing View > Display Time Format > Decimal (mm:ss.ddd).

7   Place your cursor at the beginning of the waveform and drag to the right, ending the selection at the 9 second mark. Make sure you are selecting both channels of the file by confirming that both channels are highlighted in white as you are selecting them. The Selection/View Controls (located in the bottom right corner) shows the beginning and ending points, as well as the total length of both the selection and the section of the waveform that's currently visible.

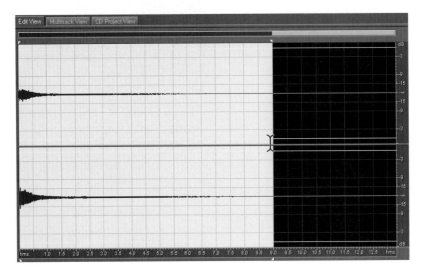

8   If you click the Play button or press the spacebar, only the selection is played. The Selection/View Controls window displays the length of your selection along with the total length of the waveform. The total length should be approximately 13.3 seconds, and the selection should be approximately 9 seconds, which is located in the End field. If necessary, adjust the length of your selection by grabbing either of the two yellow range boundaries, and slide them to the left or the right.

9   Click and drag the right range boundary (either of the yellow triangles at the top or bottom of the timeline) and drag it to the left to shorten the selection to approximately the 4.5 second mark.

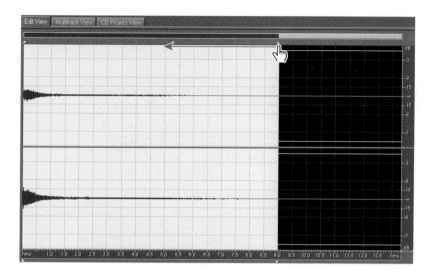

10   To keep the main crash of the cymbal and delete the silence, choose Edit > Trim. Trimming retains the information within a selection.

11   You can also delete the information within a selection. Place your cursor at the 3 second mark, click and drag to the right to select the last 1.5 seconds of the waveform. Press the Delete key on your keyboard to remove this section.

12   Press the Home key on your keyboard to return to the start of the audio file and press the spacebar to play the shortened clip. Although the sound fades out, it does not completely fade to silence. You can confirm this visually by clicking on the Zoom in Vertically button ( ) three consecutive times. The waveform is displayed larger on the screen because you are zooming into the decibel view. Note the decibel numbers on the vertical ruler along the right-hand side change as you zoom in.

13   Using the Selection/View controls as a guide, select the waveform from approximately the 2.5 second mark to the end of the clip. Choose Effects > Amplitude > Amplify/Fade. The Amplify/Fade window is displayed.

14 From the list of presets in the Amplify/Fade window choose the Fade Out option. You may have to scroll down through the list of available options to locate the Fade Out options. In the Presets section, make sure the Enable Preroll and Postroll Preview checkbox is selected and then click the Preview button. Audition will play the selection as a loop, allowing you to listen carefully to the effect. You should now hear the end of the cymbal as it fades out to silence. Uncheck the Enable Preroll and Postroll Preview checkbox and the sound of the loop changes. Preroll and Postroll Preview plays one second before the beginning of the selection (Preroll) and one second after (Postroll), and is useful for comparing the original sound with the edited version.

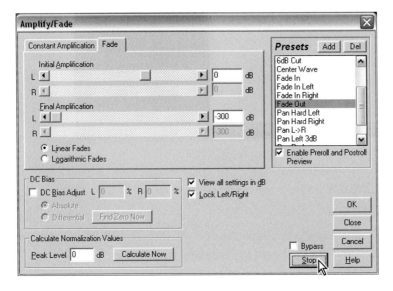

💡 *You can change the length of the preroll and postroll duration by right-clicking on the play button in the Transport Controls, and choosing Preroll and Postroll option when in the Edit View.*

15 Click OK to commit the fade out effect. The waveform fades to the zero crossing which can also be thought of as silence. Press F2 or choose Edit > Repeat Last Command to access the Amplify/Fade window. Choose Fade Out and click OK to apply the effect again. Applying the Fade effect twice creates a faster fade out.

Preroll and Postroll can also be used in the Edit View. For example, if you would like to hear the unedited version of the sound sample as it leads up to the fade out, you can do so by changing the behavior of the Play button.

16 Right-click on the Play button (▶) in the Transport Controls and choose Play Preroll and Selection. Click the Play button and Audition plays one second of the sound before the beginning of the selection. This is an extremely useful technique for previewing effects because it allows you to maintain the original selection. If you needed to make changes or add another effect you can do so.

17 Right-click on the Play button again and be sure to select the default behavior, Play from Cursor to End of View. Press the Home key to send the current-time indicator to the beginning of the session.

18 Choose File > Save from the File menu. Because we created this file as a copy at the start of this exercise, the original cymbal crash (ZildjianSizzle.cel) remains untouched.

Combining audio clips in Edit View

You can combine two or more clips in the Edit View using the Append Command. For example you can add a drum roll at the end of the loop.

1 If the last clip you worked on, ZildjianSizzle_edited.cel, is not already displayed, double-click on the file name to view the waveform.

Note: If you exited Audition after the last exercise, you will need to re-import the ZildjianSizzle_edited.cel file into the Organizer window.

2 Choose File > Open Append. The Open Append window appears. Select the file KickSnareEnding01(mono).cel from the AA_03 folder on your hard disk.

3 Inside the Open Append window be certain the Show File Information checkbox is selected. Along with other statistics, the file information indicates that this file is a monaural, as it only has one channel. The file we are appending this mono file to is a stereo file, with two channels. Audition will automatically convert the mono file to stereo.

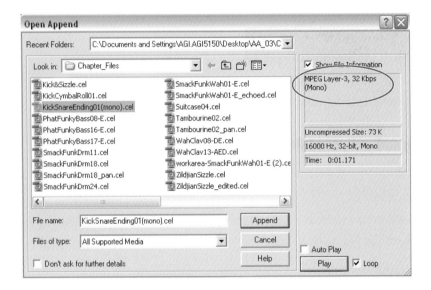

4 Click the Append button and the kick snare is added to the end of the cymbal crash. Press the spacebar to hear the new audio clip. As you listen to the clip, you should be able to hear the difference between the stereo effect of the cymbal crash and the kick snare ending. The kick snare may have come from a separate recording and does not have the same presence as the cymbal crash. You will add a reverb effect to the kick snare to change its waveform characteristics and make the sound more compatible with the cymbal crash.

5 When you appended the KicksnareEnding01(mono).cel file to the cymbal crash file, Audition added a cue in the display window, marking the insertion point of the file. The cue line is marked in red and displays the title of the inserted file. Cues are excellent ways to separate sections of a single waveform. You will be working extensively with cues in Lesson 5, Working with Loops and Waves.

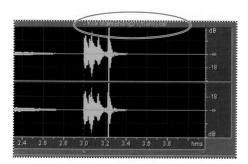

About cues

In Adobe Audition, a cue can be either a point or a range. A point refers to an exact position within a waveform (for instance, 1:08.566 from the start of the wave). A range has both a start time and an end time (for example, all of the waveform from 1:08.566 to 3:07.379). If a cue is a range, you can drag its beginning and end points to different times.

Cues have triangular handles that appear at the top and bottom of the waveform display. You use cue handles to select and adjust cues. You can also right-click a cue handle to view commands for working with cues.

—From Adobe Audition Help

6 Click the Show Cues button at the bottom of the Organizer window. You will see a change to your list of files, as a small plus sign appears to the left of the file ZildjianSizzle_edited.cel. Click on this plus sign (⊞) and the file name expands and the cue KickSnareEnding(mono) is displayed as a sublevel.

7 Double-click on the cue name KickSnareEnding(mono), and note the section of the waveform matching the original KickSnareEnding01 is automatically highlighted.

8 Press the Play to End button (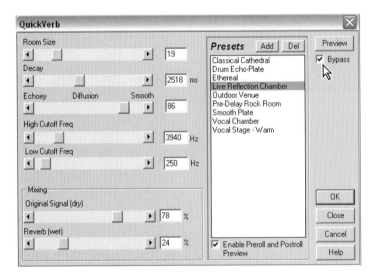) to hear the kick snare play. Click the Effects tab at the top of the Organizer window, and then click the plus sign next to Delay Effects. Double-click the Quickverb effect to open the Quickverb window.

9 Be sure the Enable Preroll and Postroll Preview checkbox is checked. From the available list of presets choose the Live Reflection Chamber and press the Preview button. You should hear the kick drum sound with Quickverb added as it loops over and over. To hear the original sound, check the Bypass checkbox. Turn off the bypass to hear the Quickverb effect again.

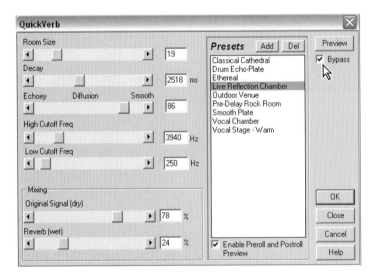

10 Click OK to apply the Quickverb effect. Press the Home key to place the current-time indicator at the beginning of the clip and then press the spacebar to hear the new file. The new clip begins with the sound of a cymbal crash and ends with the sound of a kick and snare drum.

11 Choose File > Save from the File menu.

Applying the Stereo Field Rotate effect

In the Edit View all changes you make to a waveform are permanent once you save the file. This is referred to as *destructive editing*. Non-destructive editing takes place in the Multitrack View, which you will explore in the next chapter. In addition to destructively editing a clip, changes made to files in the Edit View affect all instances of the file if it is used in the Multitrack View. If the same track is used many times in a session, one change in the Edit View will update that sample throughout the entire session.

1 In the Organizer window, click to select the Files tab and then double-click the loop tambourine02.cel to display the waveform. This file is a mono file. Click on the Effects tab and then click on the plus sign next to the Amplitude category. Certain effects are unavailable because they can only be applied to a stereo waveform. You will convert this to a stereo file.

2 Choose Edit > Convert Sample Type. The Convert Sample Type window appears. In the Channels section, click on the Stereo radio button. Make sure Left Mix and Right Mix are both at 100% and click OK.

3 The tambourine waveform now has a left and a right channel. The Amplitude effects which were previously unavailable in the Effects tab are now available. Double-click the Stereo Field Rotate effect to open the Stereo Field Rotate window.

4 In the list of presets choose Pan Left to Right and click the Preview button (Preview). You should hear the tambourine begin on the left side of your speakers/headphones and pan to the right.

Default presets are often a good place to start when adding effects. You will often want to modify the default characteristics of the effect to meet your particular needs. Before you begin modifying this effect note the x and y axis in the Stereo Field Rotate window. The x axis represents the entire timeline and starts at 0 seconds and ends at 5.3 seconds. The y axis represents the number of degrees off stereo center for both the left and right channel.

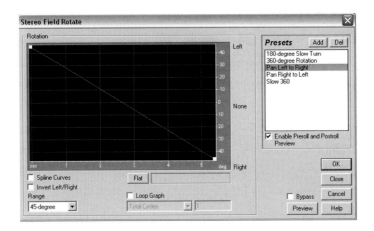

The Pan Left to Right preset pans in a linear fashion from the left to the right over a period of 5.3 seconds. Halfway through the selection the stereo effect is in the center. You will change the pan so that the transition from left to right takes place at a later point.

5   Click on the blue line at approximately the 3 second mark. An anchor point appears which you can move up the graph to the -30 degrees mark in the left channel. You can use the window beneath the graph to determine the anchor point's position in time and stereo space. Drag the anchor point to the point representing approximately 3.5 seconds and -30 degrees.

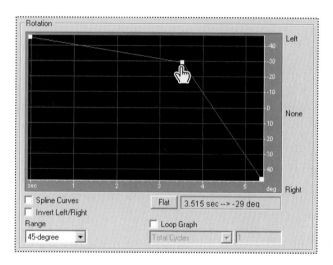

6   Preview the sound by clicking the Preview button. The tambourine stays in the left channel for a longer period of time and then quickly shifts to the right channel. When previewing the sound, note where the blue line crosses the 0 axis. This is this point that the effect is at stereo center.

If you have many anchor points on a line, you can clear all points by clicking the Flat button. This is also an excellent place to start when creating your own effects. Do not do this to the current lesson file, however.

7　Click on the checkbox named Spline Curves. The line changes from two straight lines to a curved line. This creates a smoother transition from stereo left to stereo right. Click and drag the anchor point to the right, the values should be approximately 4.5 seconds and -30 degrees. Press Preview to hear the results. Do not apply the effect yet.

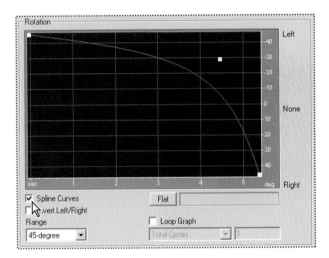

8　Before you apply the effect, click the Add button in the preset section. In the Add Preset window enter **Pan Left to Right Smooth** and click OK. Your new Stereo Field effect is added to the Presets and can be easily applied to other waveforms. Click OK again to close the Stereo Field Rotate dialog box and apply the effect.

Your waveform has now been modified to reflect the edits from this lesson. Because you started the stereo effect in the left channel, the waveform is higher than it is in the right. There is little information in the right channel at the beginning of the loop, and towards the end of the loop the waveform increases in the right channel.

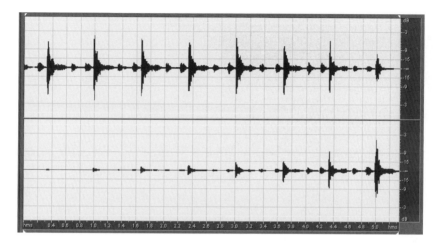

9   Click OK to close the Stereo Field Rotate window. Choose File > Save As. Navigate to the AA_03 folder on your hard disk. Name the file **Tambourine02_pan.cel** and click Save.

Note: *If an alert message appears confirming that you are overwriting an existing file, click Yes.*

Adding a favorite

As you begin to work more with Audition, you may find yourself applying the same effects repeatedly. Saving effects as favorites allows you to name and access your effects in a central location. You can even assign keyboard shortcuts to access commonly used effects.

1 In the Edit View click on the Favorites tab in the Organizer window. Click the Edit Favorites button at the bottom of the Organizer window. The Favorites window appears. Audition comes installed with certain favorites installed, such as Fade In and Fade Out.

2 Click the New button and in the Name field enter **Pan Left to Right Smooth**. In the Press New Shortcut Key field type the letter d.

3 In the Function tab, pull down the Audition Effect menu. A list of the effects available in Edit View appears, choose Amplitude/Stereo Field Rotate.

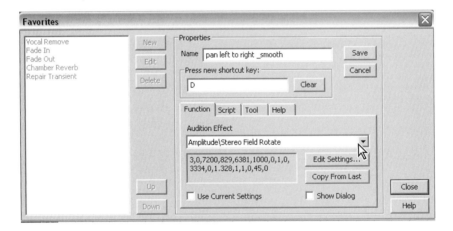

4 To ensure that the effect you are saving is the one you want, click on the Edit Settings button. The Stereo Field Rotate window appears. Click to select the Pan Left to Right Smooth preset that you saved in the previous section, and click OK. Click the save button and the favorite appears at the bottom of the Favorites list.

5 In the Favorites window, click the Up button to move your favorite to the top of the list of favorites. Click the Close button.

6 Click the Files tab to access your list of files. Double-click on the loop SmackFunkDrm18.cel to display the waveform. Press the letter **D** to apply the Stereo Field Rotate effect. You may need to wait a few moments as Audition calculates and applies the changes. When the waveform changes, the effect has been applied. Press the spacebar to hear the effect.

7   Choose File > Save As. If necessary, navigate to the AA_03 folder on your hard disk. Rename this file **SmackFunkDrm_pan.cel** and click Save.

Note: If an alert message appears confirming that you are overwriting an existing file, click Yes.

8   Press **F12** to enter Multitrack View. When working in Edit View, the Multitrack View is also open and all edits made in Edit View are automatically updated. Press the Home key and then press the Play button to hear the session. Pay particular attention to the stereo effect of the first drum clip as well as when the tambourine begins. The stereo field changes you made have been incorporated into the main mix.

9   Choose File > Save All and then choose File > Close All.

Review questions

1   How do you make a new copy of a file in the Edit View? Why is this something you would want to do?

2   What is the Preroll and Postroll Preview, and where are the options for changing them?

3   What are cues?

Review answers

1   To make a copy of a file, it must be loaded into the Edit View display window and then copied by choosing Edit > Copy to New. Creating copies of your original files is useful when you want to preserve the original sound file or create multiple versions from the same source.

2   When you apply an effect to a selection you often need to hear the original sound before and after the selection takes place. The Preroll and Postroll Preview provides one additional second to the preview. It can be enabled when you add an effect or alternatively when you press the Play or Play to End buttons in the Edit View. To change the Preroll and/or Postroll options of the play buttons, right-click the button and choose the desired command from the menu.

3   Cues mark either a specific point or a range, with a specific starting and ending point, within a waveform.

On your own

1 If you have not already previewed the Loopology collection of music clips which ship with Audition, create a new session in the Multitrack View and import two or three clips. Enter the Edit View and experiment with some of the different effects that Audition has to offer.

2 Try adding one of the Quickverb presets to a drum track. Certain effects work better on certain classes of instruments. Chorus effects work well with single instruments or voices by enriching the presence of the track. To learn more about the behavior of certain effects, use the Help button at the bottom of the Effect window to access the contextual help.

3 Change the length of the Preroll and Postroll, right-click on the Play button and choose Preroll and Postroll Options.

4 Working in the Multitrack View

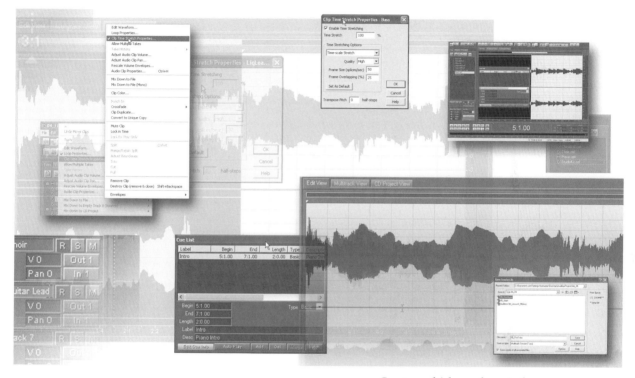

Create multi-layered musical compositions using the audio clips supplied with Adobe Audition's extensive Loopology loop library. With real time mixing, you control properties such as volume and pan. Using Audition's bus mixer, non-destructive effects such as echo can quickly be added and modified, allowing you to focus on the creative aspects of making music.

In this lesson, you'll learn how to do the following:

• Position clips within the Multitrack View.

• Control Pan and Volume envelopes.

• Add and control non-destructive effects to your multitrack session.

• Delete unneeded files and mix down a session.

• Add effects to a Bus.

Getting started

In this lesson, you'll work with a series of files in the Edit View.

1   Start Adobe Audition. If necessary, click the Multitrack View tab.

Note: If you have not already copied the resource files for this lesson onto your hard disk from the AA_04 folder from the Adobe Audition 1.5 Classroom in a Book CD, *do so now. See "Copying the Classroom in a Book files" on page 2.*

2   To play the finished session file, choose File > Open Session, and open the 04_end.ses file in the AA_04 folder, which is located within the AA_CIB folder on your hard disk. Press the Home key then play the session file by either clicking on the Play button (▶) in the Transport Controls toolbar or pressing the spacebar on your keyboard.

3   When you are ready to start working, close the 04_end.ses file by choosing File > Close All.

4   Choose File > New Session. Choose 44100 from the list of sample rates and click OK. From the File menu, choose File > Save Session As and enter the name **04_multitrack.ses**. Navigate to the AA_04 folder, located in the AA_CIB folder on your hard disk and click Save.

5   Choose File > Import. Locate the AA_04 folder and click on the file SmackFunkDrm18.cel. Click Open and it is placed into the Organizer window.

Note: Be certain to navigate to the AA_04 folder when importing the files for this chapter. Some of the file names are shared with files used in chapters two and three.

About the Multitrack View

In Multitrack View, you can add audio, video, ReWire, and MIDI files to separate tracks of a multitrack session and then mix those tracks together. When you're happy with a mix, you can export a mixdown file for use on CD, the Web, and more. Multitrack View is a flexible editing environment because mixing occurs in real time and is non-destructive. Because mixing occurs in real time, you can change mix settings during playback and immediately hear the results. For example, you can adjust a track's volume as a session plays, to properly blend the track with other tracks. Because mixing is nondestructive, mixing adjustments don't permanently change original source files. For example, you can apply four effects to a track and later remove two effects to create a different sonic texture. Adobe Audition saves information about mix settings and source files in session (.ses) files. Session files are relatively small because they contain only pathnames to source files and references to mix parameters (such as volume, pan, and effect settings). To more easily manage session files, save them in a unique folder with the source files they reference. If you later need to move the session to another computer, you can simply move the unique session folder.

—From Adobe Audition Help

Positioning clips within the Multitrack View

By default a new session opens in the Multitrack View. You will be working primarily in the Multitrack View in this session.

1   Right-click on the time display ruler that runs along the bottom of the window in the Multitrack View. From the contextual menu that appears, choose Display Time Format. From the list of time displays, choose Bars and Beats if it is not already selected.

2   If necessary, select the Files tab of the Organizer window. Double-click the SmackFunkDrm18.cel file to open it. The file opens in the Edit View. Choose View > Wave Properties. The Wave Properties window appears. Click on the Loop Info tab to access information about the source waveform. The loop option is selected, indicating that this waveform was saved as a loop rather than an individual sound sample. The original tempo of this loop, which is 98.1 beats per minute, is also displayed. Click OK to close the Wave Properties window.

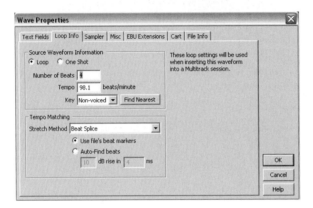

3   To hear the drum loop, click the Play Looped button (∞) in the Transport Controls, and the drum loops continuously. After listening to the loop a few times, press the Stop button (■) to stop playing the loop.

4   Click on the Multitrack View button ( ) to return to the Multitrack View. Click on the SmackFunkDrm18.cel file in the Organizer window and then click the Insert Into Multitrack button ( ) and the loop loads into track 1. Press the spacebar to hear the drum sample. When you are done previewing the sample, press the spacebar again to stop the play cursor.

5   Select the Move/Copy Clip tool ( ) and click the right edge of the drum loop to select it. Make sure your cursor changes to a double arrow (⬌) and then click and drag the loop to the right. As the end of the loop approaches a new bar, notice a thin white line appears, stretching from the top to the bottom of your display window. This line ensures that the loop is playing for a full bar. When you reach 7 bars 1 beat (7:1.00), release the mouse.

Note: If this is your first time using Audition in the Multitrack View, you may see a window informing you about the three new multitrack tools. Click OK to close the window.

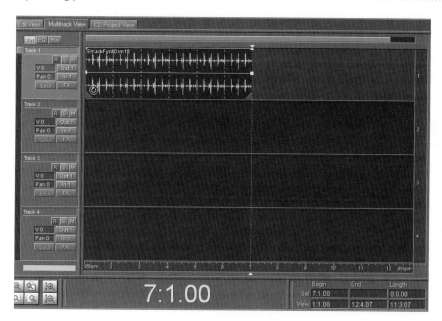

6   Click and drag the loop to 30 bars 1 beat (30:1.00). As you extend the loop, the timeline scrolls to accommodate the new length of the drum loop. When you reach the 30th bar, look for the white line to snap to the end of the clip, ensuring that it is properly aligned. Click the Zoom Out Full Both Axis button () to view the entire timeline. Because music sessions begin at 1 bar and 1 beat (1:1.00) the length of your View will be 29 bars (29:0.00). This will also be the length of your final song; the equivalent of 29 bars in decimal format is approximately one minute and ten seconds.

7 You will now load the remaining files into the Organizer window. Click on the Import File button (⬛) and the Import window appears. Confirm that you are viewing the AA_04 folder and click on Kick&Sizzle.cel, which should be the first file in the list. Next, shift-click on the last file in the list, WahClav13-AED.cel. This selects the entire range of files. Click the Open button.

Depending upon the speed of your computer, Audition may take a few moments to read the loop data. When it is done, the sound files for the session are listed in the Organizer window.

8 You will now load the guitar clip into track two. Click on the SmackFunkWah-01-E.cel loop. If necessary, press the Play button (▶) in the Organizer window to hear the guitar loop. If the Auto button (Auto) is selected the clip will play automatically. Click and hold down on the SmackFunkWah-01-E.cel loop in the Organizer window, then drag it anywhere into track 2. You can load loops into a specific track by dragging and dropping them from the Organizer window.

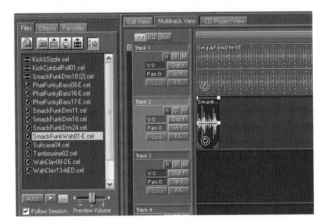

9 Select the Multitrack View button (⬛) and click the guitar clip to select it. Click again and drag the entire waveform from left to right to see how you can position a clip in time within a session. Position your guitar clip so the beginning starts at exactly 4 bars. Use the status bar at the bottom of your display to help you locate the exact bar and beat.

10 Click the handle on the bottom right corner of the guitar loop in track 2 and extend it to the right. Drag the guitar clip until the end of the loop snaps to 12 bars 1 beat (12:1.00). Notice the white line appears at every beat, not just the end of a clip. Press the Home key on your keyboard which moves the yellow current-time indicator to the beginning of the session. Press the spacebar to play the session. Note that when the guitar begins to play, it is perfectly in time with the other clip. Press the spacebar to stop playing the session.

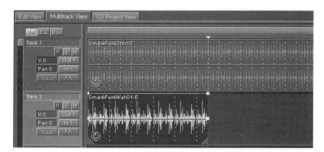

11 To add the same guitar track to the end of your song. Click and drag the SmackFunkWah-01-E.cel loop into track 2, and then position the beginning of the clip at 24 bars 1 beat (24:1.00). Place your cursor on the bottom right corner of the clip and click and drag to extend the clip. Align the end of the guitar clip with the end of the drum clip in track 1 at 30 bars 1 beat (30:1.00).

Creating a bass track

You will now add three different bass clips to create a bass track.

1 Click and drag the loop PhatFunkyBass08-E.cel into Track 3 from the Organizer window. Using the Move/Copy Clip tool, click and drag the entire sample so that it begins at the second beat (2:1.00) and then click and drag the lower right corner and extend the clip to the 6 bars 1 beat mark (6:1.00). Remember to use the white lines to help align the clip to bars and beats

2 From the Organizer window, click and drag the clip PhatFunkyBass16-E.cel into track 3 and position the beginning of the clip at 8 bars one beat (8:1.00). Click and drag the handle on the bottom right of the clip and extend the loop until it ends at 12 bars 1 beat (12:1.00).

3 Drag the clip PhatFunkyBass17-E.cel into track 3 from the Organizer window. Position the beginning of the clip at 12 bars 1 beat (12:1.00). Click and drag the handle on the bottom right of the clip to extend the loop so it ends at 20 bars 1 beat (20:1.00).

4 Drag another instance of PhatFunkybass08-E.cel into your bass track. Place the beginning at 20 bars 1 beat (20:1.00). Do not extend this clip.

5 To place your clips precisely on the timeline, you can also use the current-time indicator to align your clips. Press the Home key to ensure the current-time indicator is at the beginning of the session, it is represented as yellow triangles at the top and bottom of your tracks. Place your cursor over one of the yellow triangles until it turns into a pointing finger (☝). Click and drag the current-time indicator until the time reads (12:3.01) It is not crucial that the last two numbers are exact. You will now align the end of a clip to the current-time indicator.

6 Drag the Tambourine02.cel into track 4 and position the clip so it begins at 8 bars 1 beat (8:1.00). Click and drag the handle on the bottom right of the clip until it aligns with the current-time indicator at 12 bars 3 beats (12:3.00). The current-time indicator is useful as a guide for clips.

7 Choose the Move/Copy tool (✛) and right-click the tambourine clip while dragging the clip slightly to the right. Place the beginning of the clip at the 22 bar mark (22:1.00) and release your mouse button. A small context menu appears, choose Copy Reference Here.

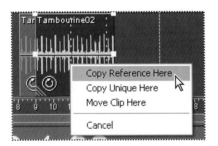

Note: *A reference copy takes up no additional space on your hard drive. Changes made to the original file also modify all reference copies based on that file. Creating a unique copy creates a separate file which is unaffected by any changes made to the original file. Creating a unique copy increases the overall size of your session, as it creates a duplicate sound file on your hard drive.*

8   Drag the Kick&Sizzle.cel clip from the Organizer window into track 4 and then position the clip to start at 16 bars 1 beat (16:1.00). Note in the Organizer window that the icon for this clip is marked as audio, this indicates that this clip has not been enabled for looping and will not extend.

You will be adding one more music track to this song. Audition is capable of using up to 128 tracks of audio.

9   To view additional tracks, click the Zoom Out Vertically button ( ). You should see at least 2 remaining tracks in this multitrack session. Drag the clip WahClav08-DE.cel into Track 5. Use the Move/Copy Clip tool to place the start of the clip at 13 bars 1 beat (13:1.00). Click on the handle on the bottom right and drag to the right to extend the clip to the 17 bars 1 beat mark (17:1.00).

10   Click and drag the WahClav13-AED.cel clip into track 5. Place the beginning of the clip at 17 bars 1 beat (17:1.00) and then click on the bottom right of the clip and drag to the right, extending the clip to 21 bars 1 beat (21:1.00).

11   Add the Suitcase04.cel clip to track 5, by clicking and dragging it from the Organizer window into this track. Place the beginning of the clip at 21 bars 1 beat (21:1.00), click on the bottom right, and drag to the right, extending the clip to 28 bars 1 beat (28:1.00). If you are having difficulty locating the exact spot on the timeline, use your current-time indicator to find the 28:1.00 mark and extend the end of the clip to the current-time indicator.

12   To add the final clip to your session, move the current-time indicator to approximately 28 bars 3 Beats (28:3.00). Drag the KickCymbalRoll01.cel from the Organizer window into track 5 and align the beginning of the clip with the current-time indicator. Adding the Cymbal Roll extends the length of the song.

Cymbal Roll clip extended.

To view all the clips in the session, click the Zoom Out Full Both Axis. Press the Home key on your keyboard to return your cursor to the beginning of the session and then press the spacebar to hear your composition. You will be adding one more basic change to the structure of the song.

13 In the Organizer window, click on the clip SmackFunkDrm24.cel. If necessary, click to select the Loop button in the Organizer window and then click the Play button in the Organizer window to hear the file. This is a drum fill, which you will add to your drum track. This breaks up the repetition of the main drum loop and propels the momentum of the song. Press the Stop button after listening to the clip. Move the current-time indicator to the 7 bars 1 beat mark (7:1.00), and then click the Zoom to Selection button (![zoom icon]).

Note: The Zoom to Selection increases the magnification of a session and centers the current-time indicator. This is very useful when working on small sections of a clip

14 Select the Time Selection tool (I) and click in the SmackFunkDrm18 clip in track 1. Click and drag to create a selection starts at 7 bars 1 beat (7:1.00) and ends at 8 bars 1 beat (8:1.00). Use the Selection/View controls to confirm your selection.

15 Choose Edit > Cut from the menu or press the Delete key on your keyboard to cut 1 bar from the main drum track.

16 Right-click on the clip SmackFunkDrm24.cel in the Organizer window and choose Insert Into Multitrack from the contextual menu. The drum fill is 1 bar long and fits perfectly into the main drum track. Move your current-time indicator to the 6 bar mark (6:1.00) and then press the spacebar to hear your composition play from this point. After the drum fill, press the spacebar to stop the session.

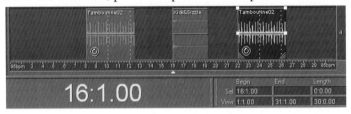

Mixing and effect basics

Creating your own composition is a matter of arranging music clips in time. Although Audition makes it simple to create multi-layered compositions using sound loops, you can modify the different tracks and instruments to create sounds and tracks that meet your needs.

1   Press the Home key to place the cursor at the beginning of the timeline and press the spacebar to play the session. As the song begins to play, click the S button (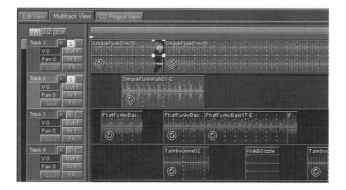) on track 1 to play only the drums in this track. The other tracks are turned off and visually grayed out. Listen to the drums for a few moments and click the Solo button again, and the other tracks return to play in real time. By using the mute and solo buttons you control which tracks are played and which tracks are silent. Allow the song to continue to play.

2   While the song is still playing, press the Solo button on track 1 again. Hold down the Control key and click the Solo button on track 2, which is the guitar track.

Holding down the Control key and clicking the Solo button allows you to solo more than one track at the same time. Click the Solo buttons on both the drum track and the guitar track to enable all your tracks, and then press the spacebar to stop playing the session.

3   Press the Home key to return the current-time indicator to the beginning of the session and then press the Play button. Press the M button in track 1, which is the drum track, to mute this track. The other tracks continue to play while this track is muted. Ctrl-click the mute button for Track 2, which is the guitar track. This turns off this track as well. Control-clicking works the same with both the Mute and Solo buttons. Click the Mute button again in track 1 and track 2 to make them audible again.

4   If your mixer is not already displayed, choose Window > Mixer and move it to the right-hand side of your screen so that it is docked to the Audition window. Click and drag the main slider down to -2. Reducing the overall volume prevents your session from sounding distorted.

When you add more instruments to a song it becomes louder. Audition can be used to control the overall session volume as well as the volume of individual tracks. You can control the volume of individual tracks in the Mixer window or directly in the track controls.

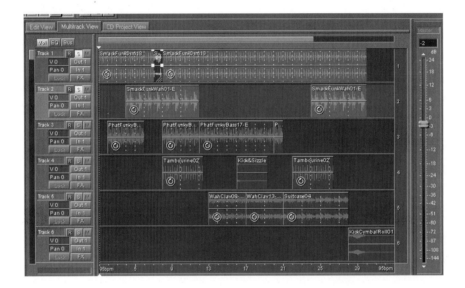

5   Press the Home key to return your current-time indicator to the beginning of the session and press the spacebar to play the session. At the top left of the Multitrack View, click on the "Vol" tab if it is not already selected. Place your cursor over the track 1 box labeled "V 0", this is the default value for the volume in this track. Click and drag to the right to raise the volume to 2.0. This increases the volume of the drums.

6   Position your cursor over the Volume box for track 2, which is the guitar track. Right-click and a volume slider window appears. Like the master mixer, you can drag the slider up to increase the volume or drag it down to decrease the volume. Raise the volume to 2 dB and click the Close Window button in the upper right corner of the [2] Vol window.

7 In addition to changing the volume of a track you can also change the pan or balance. As your session is playing, right-click on the Pan text box in track 2 and a Pan window opens.

The pan of this track is in the center, which is 0. This is the default setting. Drag the Pan slider all the way to the right, which is designated as 100. Now the guitar plays exclusively in the right channel of your speakers or headphones. Drag the slider all the way to the left, which is the -100 designation, to hear the guitar in the left channel of your speakers or headphones. Panning to either extreme has a tendency to sound artificial, so place the guitar track at -30 on the left channel.

8 Select the Mixers window by the double bar at the top of the window and drag it to the left, which detaches and floats the window. Place your cursor over the right edge of the Mixer window. When the horizontal double-arrows are displayed, click and drag to the right, expanding the size of the window. This reveals the controls for the individual tracks. Extend the window to view the first 5 tracks, although it is possible to display more tracks. This Mixer window emulates a mixing board. Notice that the volume and pan changes you made to the drum and guitar tracks are both visible.

Although controlling the pan and volume of individual tracks is fairly easy with a small session, the more tracks you add to a session, the more difficult it becomes to keep track of the individual settings. The Mixers window makes it easier to manage a larger number of tracks.

Expanded Mixers window.

9 Press the spacebar to play the session. In the Mixers window, click and drag the slider for track one toward the top. Notice that the volume of the drum track increases as you increase the volume. Move the slider to the 10 value. Wait until the organ track begins to play and then click and drag the slider for track five down to the -10 setting, reducing the volume of this track. Return the value for the first track to the value 2 and set the value for track five to 0. Press the spacebar to stop the session.

10 Move the Mixers window back to its original location by clicking the top of the window and dragging it into the right side of the screen. Notice that only the master volume remains visible after the mixer is docked.

Using volume and pan envelopes

Audition provides additional tools to dynamically change the volume and pan settings for individual clips over time.

About envelopes

With clip envelopes, you can automate volume, pan, and effects settings over time. For example, you can automatically increase clip volume during a critical musical passage and later reduce the volume in a gradual fade out. For tracks with real-time effects, you can also automatically change the ratio of dry to wet sound.

Envelopes operate nondestructively, so they don't change the original audio file in any way. If you open an original file in Edit View, for example, you won't hear the effect of any clip envelopes. Envelopes also operate in real-time, so you can edit them as a mix plays.

You can identify envelopes by color and initial position. For example, volume envelopes are green lines initially placed across the top of clips. Pan envelopes are blue lines placed in the center of clips. You edit envelopes by dragging control points on these lines. With volume envelopes, for example, the top of a clip represents 100% of track volume, while the bottom of a clip represents full attenuation (silence). With pan envelopes, the top of a clip represents full left, while the bottom represents full right. If an envelope is too high or low, preventing you from raising or lowering control points, you can rescale it.

—From Adobe Audition Help

1   Start by editing the volume envelope of the first clip in track 5, which is the organ track. Drag your current-time indicator to 12 bars 1 beat (12:1.00) and then press the spacebar to play the session. The first organ clip begins at full volume. To create a smoother transition, you will create a fade into the clip. Press the spacebar to stop playing the session.

2   Click on the WahClav08DE.cel in Track 5 with the Move/Copy Clip tool. If necessary, click Show Volume Envelopes button (📷) and also click on the Edit Envelopes button (📷) if not already selected. A thin green line with control points on either side appears at the top of the clip.

*Volume envelopes off and
volume envelopes on.*

Place your cursor over the control point on the top left side and a small tool-tip appears, indicating that the volume is at 100% or 0 dB. Click the control point and drag it down to the very bottom of the clip. As you drag, the tool-tip changes to reflect the volume level. Drag the point down to the bottom of the clip, reducing the volume of the clip to 0%, which is silent. Press the spacebar to hear the effect of the envelope. When the first organ clip is finished, press the spacebar to stop playback.

3   To provide additional control over the level of the clip, you will add a control point to the volume envelope. Place your cursor on the volume envelope line at approximately the 14 bar mark. Before clicking, confirm that you see the small plus sign, which indicates that your cursor is positioned on the line, then click to add a control point. Drag the new control point up toward the top of the clip, using the tool-tip to guide you in changing the volume to approximately 85% at the 14 bar mark. Press the spacebar to play the section again. Now, instead of a gradual fade in, the volume of the clip quickly fades in, and then becomes gradually louder.

4   Right-click on the WahClav08DE clip. From the context menu that appears, choose Envelopes > Volume > Use Splines. Your volume envelope changes to a slightly curved line. The control point is no longer on the line itself. Select the second control point and drag it upwards to the top of the clip. This causes the volume envelope to change as a logarithmic curve. Press the spacebar to play. Your fade in now sounds smoother as the transition is more gradual. After listening to the clip, press the spacebar to stop playback.

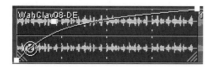

5   Select the second control point in the WahClav08DE clip and drag it up and off the clip, as if you were dragging the control point into the track positioned above the clip. This removes the control point and resets the volume envelope to its previous state. Next, select the control point on the left side and drag it back up to the top of the clip, restoring the volume to 100%.

6   You will now create a selection and allow Audition to create a fade in. Using the Time Selection tool (I), place your cursor at the beginning of the WahClav08DE, and then click and drag to the right to make a selection of two bars starting at the beginning of the clip (13:1.00) and ending at (15:1.00). Right-click on the clip and choose Crossfade > Logarithmic In from the context menu. This adds a series of control points within the selection to create a fade-in. Press the spacebar to play just the selection and to hear the fade-in. Press the spacebar to stop playing the selection.

7   You can also use Audition to create fade outs. Select the Suitcase04.cel clip in track 5 by clicking on it, then place your cursor on bar 25 and click and drag to the right to make a selection of three bars from (25:1.00) to (28:1.00). Right-click on the clip and choose Crossfade > Logarithmic Out from the context menu. This automatically creates a smooth fade out. Press the spacebar to play the selection and hear the fade-out. Press the Home key to place the current-time indicator at the beginning of the session.

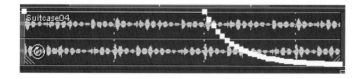

8   Envelopes can also be used to control the Pan values, which is the positioning of a sound in stereo. Click and drag the current-time indicator to the 7 bar and 1 beat mark (7:1.00). Select the Multitrack View button ( ) and click on the first tambourine clip in track 4 then click on the Show Pan Envelopes button ( ) if it is not already selected. A line with control points appears in the middle of the clip. Drag the control point on the left side to the top, starting the pan at stereo left. Drag the second control point to the bottom of the clip, causing the clip to end the pan at stereo right. Press the spacebar to play the session, and note the tambourine moves in stereo space from left to right.

Using the Effects Rack and Effects Envelopes

When working in Audition's Multitrack View, you can apply various effects to a clip and never have to worry about altering the original waveform. Additionally, effects can be controlled with envelopes, providing refined control over your sound.

1   Click on the second instance of the SmackFunkWah01-E clip in track 2 and be certain that the Vol tab is selected in the upper left corner of the Multitrack View window. Click the FX tab (   ) in Track 2 to access the Track 2 Effects Rack window.

2   You will add an echo to the end of the guitar track which will end the song. In the field for Friendly Name, type echo. In the list for Installed Real-Time effects, click on the plus sign next to Delay Effects. Select Echo and then click the Add button.

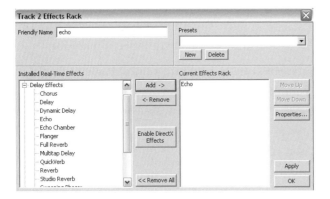

3   Click on the Properties button and the controls for echo appear. Move the sliders for both Left and Right Decay to 35% and then change the delay to 1.0 beats for both left and right channels. Click the close box in the upper right corner to exit the echo window, and then click OK to close the Effects Rack window.

4   Press the Home key to place your current-time indicator at the beginning of the timeline and then press the spacebar to listen to your session. The echo effect has been applied to the entire track. Press the spacebar to stop playing the session.

5   Click the Show Volume Envelopes button to turn off the Volume Envelopes display. The Volume Envelope line and the Wet/Dry Envelope line you are about to add share the same space at the top of the clip and it is easier to work when only one of them is displayed.

6   Enable the Wet/Dry envelopes by clicking on the Show Wet/Dry Mix Envelopes button (![Wet]). To remove the effect from the first clip, press and hold the Ctrl key and then click and drag to move the left control point in the first clip down to the bottom of the clip. Note that the second control point moves as well because holding down the Ctrl key allows you to move all envelope points in a clip in unison. After you have moved the control points, release the mouse and the Ctrl key. Press the spacebar to play the session, notice the first clip no longer has the echo effect, this is because you decreased the level of the effect to 0%.

7   You have now finished your song. Press the spacebar when done listening.

8   Choose File > Save Session, and then choose File > Close Session and its Media.

Review questions

1   What is the difference between an audio file, sometimes called a one shot and an audio loop?

2   How do you make a copy of a file in the Multitrack View? What is the difference between a Unique Copy and a Reference Copy?

3   What is the difference between controlling volume of an individual track versus controlling the volume using envelopes?

4   How do you apply a non-destructive effect to an audio track? How is the level of the effect modified?

Review answers

1   Audio loops have been configured to loop seamlessly when you bring them into the multitrack. You can visually identify music loops in the multitrack if there is a Loop icon (↻) in the clip itself. Standard music files are identified in the Organizer window and have no icon when dropped into the multitrack.

2   There are several ways to make a copy of a clip. Using the file menu, selecting a clip and then choosing Edit > Convert to Unique Copy will create a new copy of the file. Alternatively, the Move tools will also make a copy of the clip, however the behavior is different based on which tool you choose. Using the Move/Copy tool, right-click on a clip and choose either Copy Reference Here or Copy Unique Here. Copy Reference will make a copy of the clip, any changes made to the original clip will also change the copy. Copy Unique will create an independent copy, changes to the original file do not affect the unique copy. Using the Hybrid tool, right-clicking on a clip while holding the shift key will also create a unique copy.

3   Raising or lowering the volume of a track using the track properties will raise or lower the volume of all the clips in the track equally. Volume envelopes are a characteristic of every clip added to the multitrack, volume can be selectively raised or lowered on a clip-by-clip basis. In addition, Volume Envelopes allow you to dynamically raise or lower the volume, allowing you to create fade ins and fade outs, for example.

4   To add a non-destructive effect to a track, click on the FX button in the track properties. You must add the effect or effects you desire from the list of installed real time effects to the effects rack. The amount of the effect can be changed using the mixer located in the Effects window. Additionally, the Wet/Dry Envelopes can adjust the location of the effect in relation to a clip.

On your own

1   Change the mix of your saved song by opening the mixer and using the track sliders to raise or lower the individual tracks as the session is playing. Adjust the pan of the clips to place the sound of a track in stereo left or right. Pay careful attention to the level meters and make sure that the overall volume of the session is not clipping.

2   Using the Volume, Pan and Wet/Dry mix envelopes, return to the session from the previous exercise and change the envelopes on alternate clips to create a different mix. Place different instruments in the foreground and note how the song changes. Be sure to use the spline curves by right-clicking on a clip and choosing Envelopes.

3   Click the FX tab on a different track and, if need be, follow the steps in the Using the Effects Rack section to experiment with the different effects installed with Audition. Good starting points would be adding a Chorus effect to the guitar track or the Quickverb effect to the drum track.

5 Working with Loops and Waves

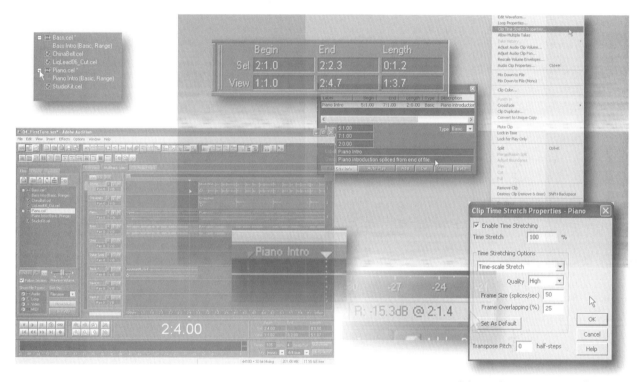

You can use Adobe Audition to view and edit waveforms using multiple views. Using specific tools, you can isolate frequencies and varying lengths of a waveform. Adobe Audition also provides powerful tools for creating, viewing and editing loops.

In this lesson, you'll learn how to do the following:

• Create a loop.

• Add a loop to a multitrack.

• Create a loop from a waveform.

• Use Cues to label and identify parts of a waveform and track.

• Change waveform properties.

• Use the Stretch effect to modify waveforms.

• Calculate and change the tempo of a file.

Getting started

In this lesson, you'll create a multitrack session from a library of loops. You will then modify properties of the loops using different methods such as the Stretch effect and Tempo. You will then modify the overall multitrack session using global features specific to the Multitrack View.

1   Start Adobe Audition. Click on the Multitrack View tab if not already selected.

2   Choose File > Open Session, and open the 05_Start.ses file within the AA_05 folder on your hard disk.

Note: If you have not already copied the resource files for this lesson onto your hard disk from the AA_05 folder on the Adobe Audition 1.5 Classroom in a Book *CD, do so now. See "Copying the Classroom in a Book files" on page 2.*

3   Choose File > Save Session As... Enter the file name **05_FirstTune.ses**, and save it in the AA_05 folder on your hard disk.

The Audition file appears completely empty. You will import several loops later in the lesson.

4   To review the finished session file, choose File > Open Session, and open the 05_End.ses file in the AA_05 folder within the AA_CIB folder. Click the Play button (▶) in the Transport Controls toolbar or press the spacebar on your keyboard to play the file.

5   When you are ready to start the lesson, close the 05_end.ses file by choosing File > Close Session and Its Media.

6   Open the 05_FirstTune.ses you just saved, by selecting File > Open session.

Adding loops to a multitrack

You will start building your session by importing five loop-enabled clips from the AA_05 folder. Two of these loops are mixed-down waveforms: piano.cel and bass.cel. This is indicated by the waveform icon (▦) next to their file names in the Organizer window. The remaining three files are loops from the Adobe Audition Loopology CD. A loop is identified by the circular icon, left of the file name (↻).

1   Choose File > Import... Select the following loops located in the AA_05 folder by Ctrl-clicking them, and then click Open to import them into the session:

• Piano.cel

• Bass.cel

• Choir.cel

• ChinaBell.cel

• StudioKit.cel

Each file is added to the Organizer window located on the left-hand side of the Audition interface.

2   Select the StudioKit.cel loop from the Organizer window by clicking on it. Drag the loop into the Multitrack View window on the right and release the loop in the Drums track. Notice that the first five tracks have already been named by instrument.

3 Repeat the previous step with the remaining loops in the Organizer window, dragging each loop onto its appropriate track.

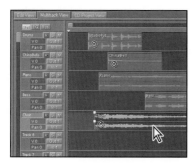

You will now align the starting position of each clip in the Multitrack View.

4 Position your mouse over the timeline across the bottom of the Multitrack View window and right-click. From the context menu, select Display Time Format and confirm that Bars and Beats is selected.

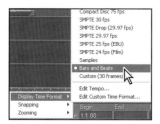

5 Right-click once again anywhere in the timeline and select Snapping. Confirm that the Snap to Ruler (Coarse) option is selected, and return to the Multitrack View window.

6   Choose the Hybrid tool (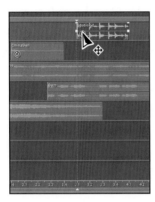) from the Multitrack toolbar at the top of the screen. Right-click on the StudioKit.cel clip in the first track and drag to move it to the point 3:1 on the timeline. Placing the clip at this location on the timeline indicates that the clip will begin to play on beat one of the third measure. Notice that as you drag your clip, snap lines appear indicating each beat in the Drums track.

7   Repeat step 6, dragging each of the remaining clips so they start at the 3:1 position on the timeline.

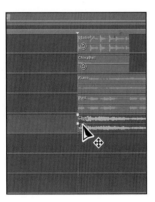

8 Save the session by selecting File > Save Session As, and select the 05_FirstTune.ses file in which you are currently working. In the Save window that appears, select the Save copies of all associated files option in the lower left hand corner. If necessary, navigate to the AA_05 folder on your hard disk, and then click the Save button, then click Yes to overwrite the file.

The Save copies of all associated files option packages all loops and waveforms into the same folder as the file you are currently saving. This option makes it easy to transfer Adobe Audition session files from one computer to another by ensuring that all your component files are located in the same location as your .ses file.

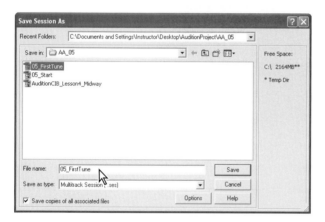

9 Click the Play button (▶) in the Transport Controls toolbar to listen to the session. You can also play the session by pressing the spacebar.

Creating a loop

You will now extend the length of a loop using Audition's Loop tool. This is done without modifying the original loop based file. The loop will simply be repeated within your multitrack session.

The Piano and Bass track both play longer than the Drum track. You will now extend the StudioKit.cel clip so the drums play through most of the session.

1   Click the Zoom Out Full Both Axis button () in the Zoom Controls toolbar, located at the bottom of the screen ,to view the entire timeline. Click on the StudioKit.cel clip in the Drums track to select it, then position your cursor over the lower right hand corner of the clip. The cursor now changes into the Loop tool (⁑). Click the bottom right corner of the clip and drag to the right, stopping when the end of the clip is at the 9:1 position on the timeline.

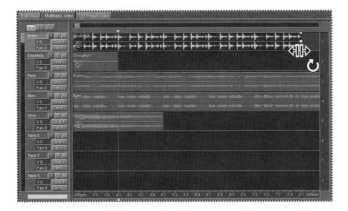

If necessary, click the Rewind button (⏪) in the Transport Controls window and then click the Play to End of File button (⏺) to hear your changes. The loop now continues to play over the Piano and Bass track as it repeats itself.

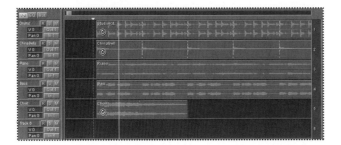

2   Repeat step 1, extending the ChinaBell.cel clip, causing it to continue to play at the same time the Piano, Bass, and StudioKit clips are playing.

3   Press the Home key on your keyboard to move the current-time indicator to the start point of your session, then preview your new file by pressing the Play to End of File button (⏺).

Making a loop from a larger waveform

Next you will create a new loop by isolating parts of a larger loop. You will then save the isolated portion as a unique file, which you will incorporate into the multitrack session.

1   Click the Edit View tab to enter the Edit View. Click the Import File button () in the Organizer window. If necessary, navigate to the AA_05 folder on your hard drive. Select the LiqLead03.cel file and then hold down the Ctrl key on your keyboard and also select the LiqLead06.cel file. Click the Open button to import these two files into the Organizer window.

Preview each of these files in the Organizer window by clicking on each file name and clicking the Play button (▶) at the bottom of the Organizer window. If the Loop button is selected, you may need to click the Stop button to stop playback.

2   Double-click the LiqLead06.cel file in the Organizer window to view the waveform.

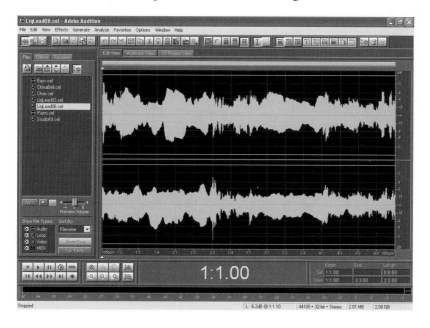

You will now isolate the beginning portion of this loop and use it within your Multitrack session file.

3   Play the loop by pressing the spacebar. Notice the play cursor as it travels left to right.

4   Play the loop again, noticing the location of the play cursor as the loop makes a musical run of notes. The musical run pauses on a long tone before rising again into another long run of notes. You should notice this point at approximately the 3:1 point within the loop.

5   Click and drag the current-time indicator (▣) to position 3:1 on the timeline.

6   Choose the Time Selection tool (⛭). Position your cursor over the center divider of the Edit View window at the 3:1 location. Click and drag to the right, towards the end of the clip. This area becomes selected.

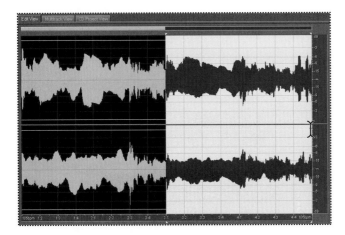

7   Press the Delete key, removing the selected portion of the clip. Press the Home key and then review the remaining portion of the loop by pressing the spacebar on your keyboard to play the clip.

8 Select View > Wave Properties to open the wave properties window, and click on the Loop Info tab. Input **8** as the Number of Beats value and then click OK.

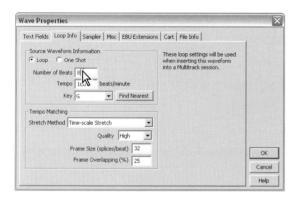

9 Save this new loop by choosing File > Save As. Name the file **LiqLead06_Cut.cel**, making certain to save this file within the AA_05 folder on your hard disk. A message appears asking if you want to overwrite this file, click Yes.

Note: *While working in the Edit View, Adobe Audition acts as a waveform editor. Actions and save commands in the Edit View only affect the loop in which you are working and not the entire Adobe Audition Session.*

10 Click the Multitrack View tab to view your session file once again.

The LiqLead06.cel file is replaced by the LiqLead06_Cut.cel file in your Organizer window. As an individual and unique loop, it is now ready to be used in a Multitrack session.

11 Click and drag the LiqLead06_Cut.cel file from the Organizer window onto Track 6 of the multitrack session. If you cannot see Track 6 of the multitrack, click the Zoom Out Full both Axis button (🔍).

12 Click the title area of the Track Controls for Track 6 to select this area. Rename the Track 6 title as **Guitar Lead**.

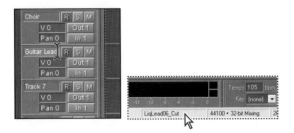

To view the clip position, use the Data Under Cursor toolbar option. Choose View > Status Bar > Show and confirm that the Data Under Cursor option is selected. If it is not selected, choose this option.

Note: *The Data Under Cursor position, located below the level meters bar indicates your current cursor position as you move a loop within the multitrack session. A loop may also be identified by its title in this toolbar by mousing over the loop in the Multitrack View.*

13 Right-click and drag the LiqLead06_Cut.cel clip to position it at the start of the multitrack session. Confirm that it is at the 1:1.00 position after it is placed in the multitrack session.

14 Select File > Save Session.

Changing waveform properties

In your session file, the Guitar Lead track is substantially louder than the other tracks. As this track is playing, the Level Meter indicates that your session comes very close to 0dB. This would result in a clipped audio signal. You will use several of Audition's effects to normalize and alter the loops in this session, resulting in a more balanced session.

1   Double-click the LiqLead06_cut.cel loop in the Organizer window. The loop opens in the Edit View.

Notice that the waveform contains many peaks which reach just under the -4dB level in both channels. You will reduce the overall amplitude of this waveform to blend it more smoothly into the multitrack session with other loops on tracks 1 through 5.

2   Right-click between both left and right channels and choose the Select Entire Wave option. The entire waveform is highlighted from start to finish.

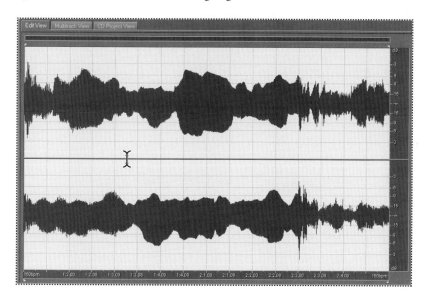

3 Select the Effects Tab from the Organizer window and click on the plus sign (⊞) to the left of the Amplitude option. This reveals all the available effects that relate to amplitude.

4 Double-click on the Normalize option and the Normalize window opens. In the Normalize window, confirm that the option for Normalize L/R Equally is selected. Select the option for "Normalize to" and insert **25** as the increment and then click OK. This effectively reduces the amplitude of the selected waveform to 25%.

5 Preview the file by pressing the spacebar or clicking the Play button (▶). Notice that the peaks of the waveform now fall well below the -9dB level, resulting in the reduced volume (amplitude) of the file.

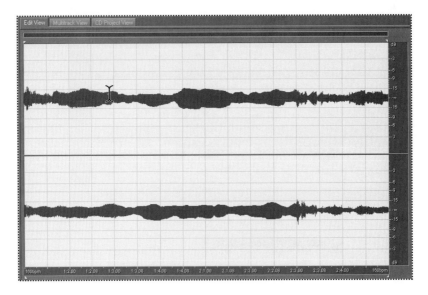

6 Select File > Save, overwriting the LiqLead06_Cut.cel loop.

7 Click on the Multitrack View button (▦) in the upper left of the Adobe Audition window or press the number 9 on your keyboard to switch to the Multitrack View.

8 Press the Home key and then play the session by pressing the spacebar on your keyboard. Note that your loop has been updated to reflect the changes you just made to the LiqLead06_Cut.cel loop.

9 Select File > Save Session and leave the session file open.

Using Cues

Cues are markers that label sections of a loop or waveform. Adobe Audition uses four different types of cues. Basic and Beat cues are used when isolating particular points or sections of a waveform or loop. Track and Index cues catalog multiple tracks and mark the start and end points for the creation of CDs.

You will start by isolating an interlude in both the Piano and Bass tracks to be used elsewhere in your multitrack session. By creating a unique loop of the selection, it can then be placed into the session and also repeated as an original loop.

1 Double-click the Piano.cel loop in the Piano track, opening it in the Edit View.

2 Select Window > Cue List to open the Cue List window.

3   Move the current-time indicator to the 5:1 position in the loop. Place your cursor over the waveform then click and drag to the right, selecting the remainder of the waveform.

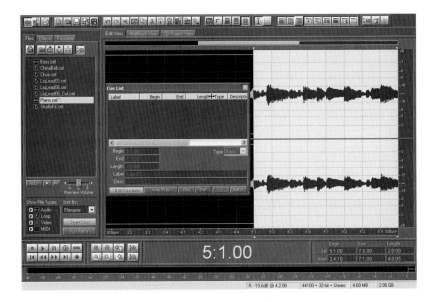

4   Click the Add button (![Add]) in the Cue List window.

5   Select the Edit Cue Info button (![Edit Cue Info]) in the Cue List window, revealing the specific properties of the cue you've just created relating to its position in the waveform.

6   Click into the "Label" area at the bottom of the Cue List window and enter **Intro** as the new label title.

7   Click into the "Desc" area at the bottom of the Cue List window and enter **Piano Intro** as the cue description.

8   Create an Intro cue for the Bass.cel loop. Do this by repeating steps 1-7 after double-clicking in the Bass.cel loop in the Organizer window. Enter **Intro** as the new label and **Bass Intro** as the cue description for this Bass Intro cue.

9   Click on the Multitrack View tab to view the session. Select the Files tab in the Organizer window.

Notice that the Piano.cel and Bass.cel files both now contain the cues you've created. This is indicated by the plus sign (⊞) to the left of each .cel file name in the Organizer window. Clicking the plus sign reveals any cues which have been saved into the .cel files. These cues can be incorporated into your multitrack as independent portions of the larger waveform.

10   Click the plus sign in the Piano.cel loop, revealing the Intro cue you've just saved. Click on the Intro cue and drag it into the very beginning of the Piano track. Right click on the file as you drag it towards the left, releasing it at the 1:00.00 position.

11   Click the plus sign in the Bass.cel loop, revealing the Intro cue you've just saved. Click on the Intro cue and drag it into the very beginning of the Bass track. The individual cue is now displayed as a separate waveform in the Multitrack View. Right click on the file as you drag it towards the left, releasing it at the 1:00.00 position

By creating cues you can more effectively select and work with sections of files, rather than having to work with the entire file.

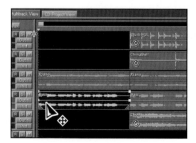

12   Choose File > Save All.

Using the Stretch method to modify waveforms

The Stretch method alters the properties of a waveform over time. For example, you can change the length of a waveform without altering its pitch. Another option allows for the manipulation of time and pitch. This effect sounds like a recording played faster than its typical speed. In this exercise you will use Adobe Audition's stretch method of loop manipulation.

1   Select the LiqLead03.cel file in the Organizer window. Click and drag the file into Guitar Lead track of your multitrack session. Release the clip immediately following the LiqLead06_Cut.cel file. Right-click and drag the file into position.

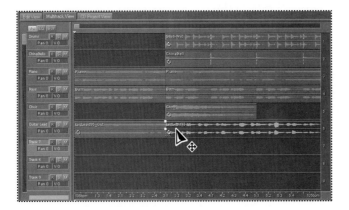

2   Confirm the LiqLead03.cel clip is selected in the session. Choose Edit > Clip Time Stretch Properties… to open the Time Stretch Properties window.

3   In the Clip Time Stretch Properties window, select the Enable Time Stretching option checkbox. In the drop-down menu within the Time Stretch Options portion of this window, confirm that the Time-scale Stretch option is selected. Enter **50** for the Time Stretch percentage and select OK.

Note: *Adobe Audition's Time-scale Stretch option resamples the loop down to a percentage of its original length. This percentage is a fraction of its length in time, while maintaining all tonal properties of the original loop.*

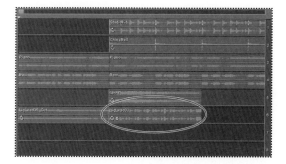

4   Click onto the end of the LiqLeadG03.cel clip in the session and drag it to position 7:1 on the time scale. This causes the loop to repeat itself once again in your session file.

5   Listen to your session by selecting the Play button (▶)from the Transport Controls toolbar or by pressing the spacebar.

Wrapping up

In order to complete the track with the LiqLead clips, you will duplicate the LiqLead06_Cut.cel and place a copy of this clip at the end of the LiqLead03.cel clip which currently ends at 7:1.

1 Select the Multitrack View button ( ) from the Multitrack Tools toolbar or by pressing V on your keyboard.

2 While pressing the Ctrl-key, right-click on the LiqLead06_Cut.cel clip and drag it to position 7:1 on the multitrack session. A duplicate icon ( ) appears over the loop as you do this, indicating a copy is being created as you drag the loop to another position in the session, leaving the original unchanged.

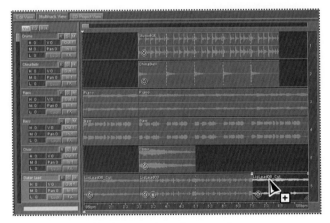

3 Play your file by pressing the spacebar.

4 Save the session by selecting File > Save All.

Changing the tempo of a file

Tempo is measured in beats per minute (bpm). This can be calculated by counting the number of beats in a loop or waveform over a span of one minute. Changing the tempo of individual waveform files in Adobe Audition is accomplished using any one of several methods. The tempo of multiple waveforms used in the same multitrack session can also be changed by using Audition's tempo toolbar. In this section you will change the tempo of your session file using settings in the Multitrack View.

1   Confirm that the Session Properties toolbar is visible by selecting Window > Session Properties. From the Session Properties window in the lower right, click on the Advanced... button (Advanced...) and select the Tempo tab.

2   Enter **110** as the new value for beats/minute. This becomes the new tempo for your multitrack session. Click OK to initiate the tempo change in Audition. Wait until the progress windows show that the change has been completed.

3   Press the spacebar and listen to your modified session file.

4   Select File > Save Session.

Review questions

1   What differences are there between simply pressing the spacebar, and using the Play controls from the Transport Controls toolbar?

2   How is a loop-enabled file identified in Adobe Audition in the Multitrack View and in the Organizer Window?

3   What difference is there in using File > Save Session from Multitrack View or File > Save As in Edit View?

4   How could you ensure that all your session files are saved in one central location on your hard disk?

Review answers

1   By default, the spacebar will play your visible session data from the Play bar to the end of your screen. Selecting the Play button from the Transport Controls toolbar will accomplish the same. Utilizing the Play to End button will play to the very end of your total session file.

2   A loop-enabled file is identified both in the Organizer Window and in the Multitrack View by the loop icon (↻).

3   The File > Save Session command while in Multitrack View will simply save the session file. Using the File > Save command while in the Edit View affects the file currently visible in Edit View. Be aware that the shortcuts are the same while in both views (Ctrl+S), so be aware of the particular view you are in.

4   While in Multitrack View, and performing a File > Save Session As, confirm that the Save copies of all associated files option is checked. This ensures that copies of all session files are saved in the same directory as the Adobe Audition Session (.ses) file.

On your own

Extend the StudioKit.cell clip to several times its length and duplicate each track several times in order to create a longer multitrack session. Then modify the amplitude of the LiqLead03.cel clip to better balance out the entire session file, using Audition's Effects menu. Place the Choir.cel loop randomly throughout your session file to break up each verse accordingly. Select File > Save Session when done with all your changes. Be sure to play your completed file!

6 | Using Noise Reduction Filters

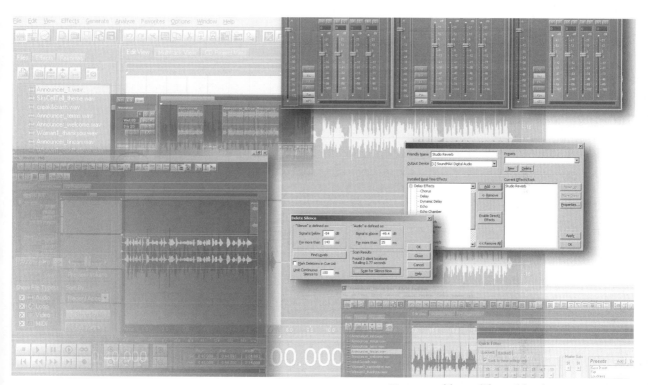

You can add new life to old or low quality audio recordings using Adobe Audition's enhancement and restoration effects. Distracting hiss or background noise can easily be removed with the Noise Reduction effect. Pops, clicks and crackles can be identified and removed using Audition's Spectral View.

In this lesson, you'll learn how to do the following:

• Navigate through Audition's Effects tab.

• Apply effects to loops.

• Save effects settings.

• Create and save a noise reduction profile.

• Remove pops, crackles and hiss from a recording.

• Use Parametric and Graphic Equalizers.

Getting started

In this lesson, you will be utilizing Adobe Audition's built-in effects to improve the overall quality of a waveform. Because many recordings do not take place in a sound booth or professional recording studio, noise is typically recorded along with the focus of your recording. Noise can be described as underlying frequencies, usually at lower amplitudes, which are picked up by the microphone during the recording session. Street noise, crowd noise, and the buzz of nearby electronic devices—such as a fan, are all examples of noise which can be recorded unintentionally.

Noise and imperfections in a recording may also be related to the recording source. Creating a digital loop from an analog source, such as a record player, may result in crackles or pops throughout the recording, due to scratches or imperfections in the vinyl record itself.

In this lesson you will use some of the tools available in Adobe Audition for repairing or removing audio imperfections.

1   Start Adobe Audition and click on the Multitrack View tab, if not already selected.

2   Choose File > Open Session, and open the 06_Start.ses file in the AA_06 folder, which is located in the AA_CIB folder on your hard disk.

Note: If you have not already copied the resource files for this lesson onto your hard disk from the AA_06 folder on the Adobe Audition 1.5 Classroom in a Book *CD, do so now. See "Copying the Classroom in a Book files" on page 2.*

3   Choose File > Save Session As, and name the file **06_Recording.ses**, and save it in the AA_06 folder.

4   To review the finished session file, choose File > Open Session, and open the 06_end.ses file in the AA_06 folder, which is located within the AA_CIB folder on your hard disk. Play the session file by either clicking on the Play button () in the Transport Controls toolbar, or pressing the spacebar on your keyboard.

5   When you are ready to start working on the lesson, close the 06_end.ses file by choosing File > Close Session and Its Media.

6   Select File > Open Session to reopen the 06_Recording.ses file you created in the previous steps.

Tools to clean up sound

The lesson files in this chapter are modeled after an amateur radio commercial demo. The Voice Over track recording was created using a low–quality microphone in a non-studio environment. The Guitar track is a sampled loop recorded from an old heavily used vinyl record. As you play this session file, note all the residual noise which is evident throughout the session. Listen to each track individually by clicking on the Solo button ( ), then pressing the spacebar on the keyboard to play.

Notice that the Voice Over track has a substantial amount of noise in the background of the recording. The Guitar track contains hiss, pops and clicks throughout the loop as a result of the wear in the vinyl record.

Audition offers several effects which can be utilized to repair these imperfections. These tools are available in the Edit View. Any change made to these files within the Edit View are destructive and will require that the changes be saved. You can also save the file using a new file name by choosing the File > Save As command.

Creating a noise reduction profile

Using Audition's Noise Reduction Profile feature you will isolate the background noise from the Voice Over sample. You will use this noise reduction profile as a filtering effect throughout the entire recording.

1   Double-click into the VoiceOver_Take1.cel loop located in the multitrack in the Voice Over track. This opens the file in the Edit View.

2   Press the Home key and then click the Zoom to Selection button (🔍) once to zoom in slightly. When you previewed the file you may have noticed a slight pause before the subject begins speaking. The file contains approximately 1 second of background noise during this pause. Isolate the first second of this waveform by clicking and dragging in the Edit View display window. Your selection should end prior to any significant change in the waveform.

3 Click on the Effects Tab in the Organizer window. Select the plus sign (⊞) positioned to the left of the Noise Reduction effect. The effect expands, revealing options.

4 Double-click on the Capture Noise Reduction Profile option from the Organizer window. If an Alert window opens, informing you that a profile is being created from the current selection, click OK. A window appears illustrating Audition's progress in creating the profile, and then the window closes after the profile is created.

5 Click anywhere in the waveform to clear the current selection and then press the Home key to place the current-time indicator at the beginning. Double-click the Noise Reduction effect in the Organizer window. The Noise Reduction effect window is displayed.

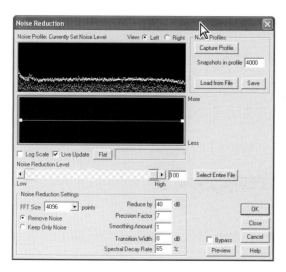

6   In the Noise Reduction effect window, click the Select Entire File button to select the entire recording, then select the Preview button to listen to the file as you make changes. Allow the file to continue to play.

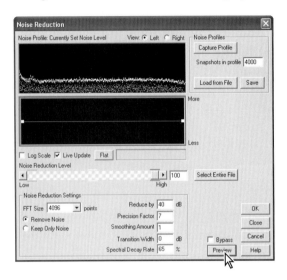

7   As you move the Noise Reduction Slider left to right, make note of its effect on the file. Move the slider to the 75% position or click into the input area and enter **75** as the value. Allow the file to continue to play.

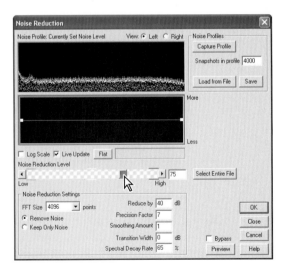

8   Click the Spectral Decay Rate field at the bottom of the window and enter **25** as the value. Click the Bypass option to hear the original file. Click Bypass again to restore the effect. The background noise is much less prominent.

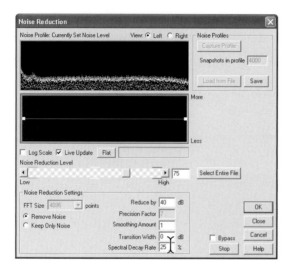

9   Click OK to close the Noise Reduction window and apply the changes to the entire waveform. Choose File > Save As to save the revised Voice Over_Take1 file.

In the Save As window, enter the name **VoiceOver.cel** and then click the Save button. Click Yes to overwrite the original file with the same name.

To reduce noise added by a sound card during recording, start the recording with one second of silence. After recording is complete, use that silence as the Noise Reduction Profile. You can then remove the identifiable noise from the finished recording. In some cases, this process can increase dynamic range by a full 10 dB.

10   Press the F12 key to switch to the Multitrack View, and then play the session file using the spacebar on your keyboard or use the Play button in the Transport Controls.

11   Save your session by selecting File > Save Session.

Removing pops, crackles, and hiss

Pops and clicks are artifacts which can be unintentionally recorded from an outside source. They may also be the result of an audio file having been cut and looped. The GuitarRiff_from_Vinyl loop, which is part of the Guitar track, contains several clicks which you will remove using Audition's Pop/Click Eliminator effects.

1   Click the Files tab to display the Organizer window. Double-click on the GuitarRiff_from_Vinyl.cel file in the Organizer window to open this file in the Edit View.

2   Preview the file by pressing the spacebar, making note of the audible pops and clicks and their connection to the large spikes in the waveform.

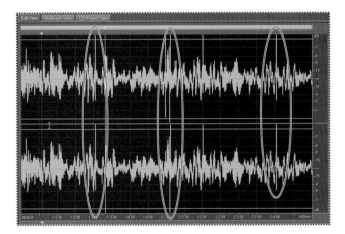

3   Click onto the Effects tab in the Organizer window. Within the Effects Tab, click the plus sign (⊞) for Noise Reduction to reveal the Noise Reduction effects, if necessary. Double-click the Click/Pop Eliminator effect, opening the Click/Pop Eliminator window.

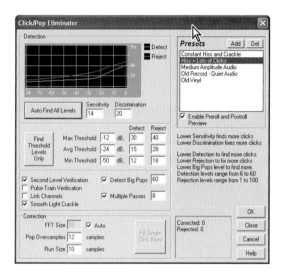

4   Select the Old Record—Quiet Audio option from the Preset portion of the window, then click the Find Threshold Levels Only button. This creates a threshold for minimum, average and maximum decibels (dB).

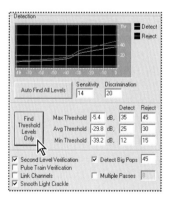

5   For each threshold value, input a new Reject value of **15**, causing Audition to isolate more clicks.

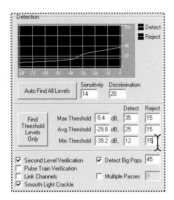

6   Save your options as a preset by clicking on the Add button in the upper right corner of the Click/Pop Eliminator window. Enter **Old_Vinyl** as the name for the preset and then click the OK button.

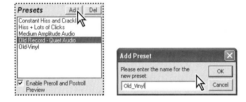

7   In the Click/Pop Eliminator window, click the OK button to initiate the changes to the GuitarRiff_from_Vinyl file.

8   Play the modified file by pressing the Play button in Transport Controls or use the spacebar on your keyboard.

9   Select File > Save As. If necessary, navigate to the AA_06 folder on your hard disk. Name the file **GuitarRiff.cel** and then click the Save button. Click Yes to overwrite the original file with the same name.

Using the Auto Click/Pop Eliminator effect

If you need to quickly remove crackle and static from vinyl recordings, first try the Auto Click/Pop Eliminator effect. You can easily select and correct a large area of audio, or a single click or pop. This effect provides the same processing quality as the Click/Pop Eliminator effect, but it offers simplified controls and a helpful preview.

At this point the guitar sample has been modified significantly. You should notice dramatic improvements in the overall quality of the recording. Using some more specific effects tools, you will now isolate and eliminate the hiss which remains. You will also remove the remaining pop located midway through the loop.

10 From the Effects options in the Organizer Window, double-click the Hiss Reduction effect. The Hiss Reduction window opens.

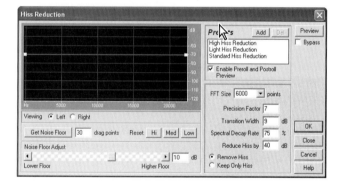

11 In the Presets portion of the window, select the High Hiss Reduction setting, then click on the Preview button to hear your changes. Allow the file to continue to play.

12 Drag the Noise Floor Adjust slider toward the right until a setting of approximately 10dB is achieved.

You can also manually enter values by clicking into the input box and entering the value from your keyboard.

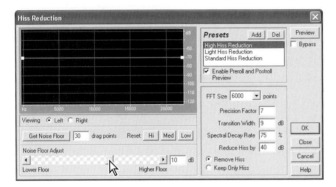

13 Click the OK button to confirm your changes, and then choose File > Save to save the revisions to the GuitarRiff_from_Vinyl file.

14 Select View > Spectral View, to display the spectral analyzer. Spectral View displays a waveform by its frequency components.

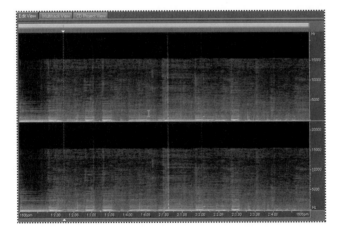

In the Spectral View, the x-axis (horizontal) represents time and the y-axis (vertical) measures frequency. This view lets you analyze audio data to see which frequencies are most prevalent. The greater a signal's amplitude component within a specific frequency range, the brighter the displayed color. Colors range from dark blue, indicating that the frequencies are very low in amplitude, to bright yellow, indicating that the frequencies are high in amplitude.

15 Press the spacebar on your keyboard to play the file. Notice that the pop correlates to the large spike indicated in the spectral view at around beat 2:4 of the waveform.

16 In the timeline, right-click and then drag to zoom into the area of the pop. Select the pop in the Spectral View window by left-clicking and dragging, to make the selection.

Note: *If you zoomed into an incorrect view, you can click the Zoom Out Full Both Axis button to expand the view. You can also right-click in the timeline and choose Zooming > Zoom Full.*

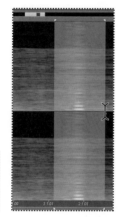

 To select noise in a specific frequency range, use the Marquee Selection tool ( ).

17 Double-click the Click/Pop Eliminator effect in the Organizer window. The Click/Pop Eliminator window opens.

18 In the Click/Pop Eliminator window, select the Old-Vinyl Preset you previously saved. This is located in the Presets portion of the window. Keep the Click/Pop Eliminator window open.

19 Select the Fill Single Click Now button. This repairs an individual click. Press OK to confirm your changes and close the Click/Pop Eliminator window.

Repairing single clicks

The Favorites tab in the Organizer window contains several effect presets. The Repair Transient preset is an effective tool for repairing single clicks or pops in an waveform. In the Edit View, make your selection, then select the Favorites tab in the Organizer window. Double-click on the Repair Transient option and Audition will repair the single instance in the waveform.

To toggle back to the waveform view, click on the Waveform/Spectral View toggle button (🖼) located in the toolbar. The zoom magnification is shared between these two views. Use the Zoom tools to change the magnification level.

20 Choose File > Save to save your changes.

Using Parametric and Graphic Equalizer to change sound quality

The Parametric Equalizer provides maximum control over tonal equalization. Unlike the Graphic Equalizer, which provides a fixed number of frequencies and Q bandwidths, the Parametric Equalizer gives you complete control over frequency, Q, and gain settings. For example, you can simultaneously reduce a small range of frequencies centered around 1,000 Hz, boost a broad low-frequency shelf centered around 80 Hz, and insert a 60 Hz notch filter.

The Graphic Equalizer allows for modification of specific frequencies. By isolating typical frequencies produced by the human voice, the recorded VoiceOver.cel file can be improved using Adobe Audition.

1 In the Organizer window, click to select the Files tab. Double-click the VoiceOver.cel file, opening the file in the Edit View.

2 Click on the Effects tab of the Organizer window and, if the waveform is not selected, choose Edit > Select Entire Wave.

3 In the Effects window click the plus sign (⊞) to the left of Filters. Double-click the Graphic Equalizer option, and the Graphic Equalizer window is displayed.

4 In the Graphic Equalizer window activate the Bypass option by clicking the check box. Select the Preview button to play your file.

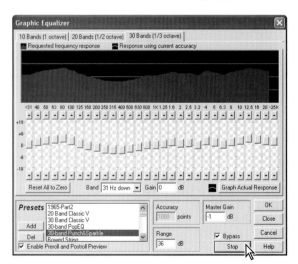

5 Click the Stop button to stop the playback of the file. Click the Bypass checkbox to deselect this option. By default, the Graphic Equalizer automatically selects a preset. Choose the Bypass option and the preset is ignored, so you hear the original file.

6 In the Presets portion of the window, select the Sloping Low End Boost option. It may be necessary to scroll down through the list of presets to locate this option. Click the Preview button to play the file with the graphic equalization effects applied. At this point you should notice an increase in the lower frequencies of the voice, resulting in a broader, fuller sound. Click the Stop button, then click OK.

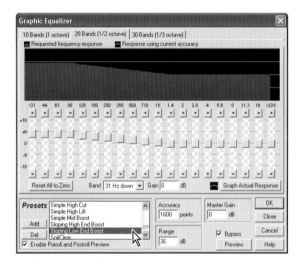

7 Select File > Save to save your changes to the VoiceOver.cel file.

8 Click on the Multitrack View button (⊞) to view your session. Preview your file by clicking on the Play to End of File button (▣) or pressing the spacebar. When you have finished listening to your file select File > Save Session.

💡 *Preview buttons in Effects windows change to Stop buttons during playback of .wav files. You may also utilize the spacebar to toggle playback of files if the Preview button is active.*

Review questions

1   What are some typical causes of noise and artifacts in sound files?

2   How can you set up a recording to later eliminate any existing background noise from the session?

3   What are the major differences between Graphic and Parametric Equalizer effects?

4   Can equalization effects be used in both Edit and Multitrack Views in Audition?

Review answers

1   Electronic equipment, poor recording source, or improper loop creation are some typical examples.

2   Allow for at least one second of silence at the very start of your recording. You can use this to build a Noise Reduction Profile which can be used later for the entire waveform.

3   Graphic Equalizers provide a fixed number of frequencies and bandwidths, whereas a Parametric Equalizer allows for control of gain, Q, and frequency.

4   Not all equalization effects are available in both the Edit and Multitrack views. When using an equalization effect in Edit View, it is considered destructive editing, as the waveform is physically altered from its original state. Introducing an effect in Multitrack View maintains the settings of the effects as being a process of the multitrack session, separating them from the waveform itself.

On your own

The graphic nature of the FFT (Fast Fourier Transform) Filter effect makes it easy to draw curves or notches that reject or boost specific frequencies. This effect can produce broad band-pass filters such as high- and low-pass filters (to maintain high and low frequencies, respectively), narrow band-pass filters (to simulate the sound of a telephone call), or notch filters (to eliminate very narrow frequency bands).

In order to round out the session file in a final step, an FFT Filter allows for the limiting of higher frequencies over an entire wave file. Reducing these frequencies helps to push the file farther into the background of our session file, leaving the Voice Over track as the main focus.

Note: The noise level of the FFT Filter effect is lower than that of 16-bit samples, so it introduces no noise when processing audio at 16-bit resolution or lower.

1   In the Files tab of the Organizer window, double-click the GuitarRiff.cel file, opening it in Edit View.

2   Click to select the Effects tab in the Organizer window.

3   Select the FFT Filter option from the Filters menu in the Organizer Window by double-clicking.

4   In the Presets portion of the window, scroll down and select The Club Downstairs preset. Click OK.

5   Preview the file by pressing the spacebar or clicking the Play button.

6   Save the file by choosing File > Save.

7 | Editing Voices

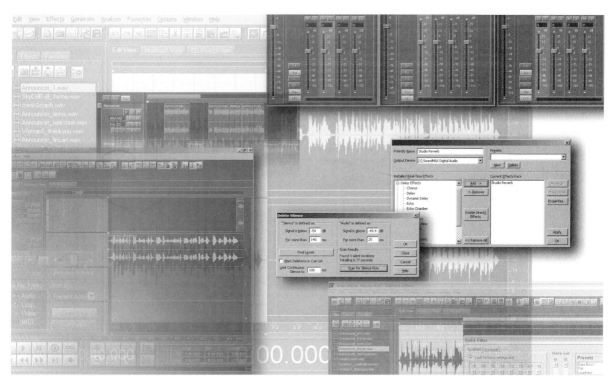

Audition's editing tools make it possible to produce professional quality audio recordings. Use Audition to delete silence and apply reverb to enhance your recordings. You can also use the Bus Mixer for refined control over the final audio mix.

In this lesson, you'll learn how to do the following:

• Split clips and save selections from master clips.

• Work with and manipulate vocal tracks.

• Use the Delete Silence feature.

• Use the Bus mixer.

• Add an effect with the Quick Filter.

Getting started

In this lesson, you'll work with a series of files in the Edit View.

1   Start Adobe Audition. Click on the Multitrack View tab.

2   To play the finished session file, choose File > Open Session. Open the 07_end.ses file in the AA_07 folder, which is located within the AA_CIB folder on your hard disk. Play the session file by either clicking on the Play button (▶) in the Transport Controls or press the spacebar.

3   When you are ready to start working, you can close the 07_end.ses file by choosing File > Close All.

4   Choose File > Open Session, and open the 07_start.ses file in the AA_07 folder, which is located in the AA_CIB folder on your hard disk.

Note: If you have not already copied the resource files for this lesson onto your hard disk from the AA_07 folder from the Adobe Audition 1.5 Classroom in a Book *CD, do so now. See "Copying the Classroom in a Book files" on page 2.*

5   Choose File > Save Session As, and name the file **07_RadioAd.ses**, and save it in the AA_07 folder.

Splitting clips and saving selections

In this exercise you will arrange several clips in your multitrack to create a radio commercial. You will use Audition's editing and processing tools to create a session which is exactly one minute in length. Commercial scripts are rarely read live. Different actors may read their parts at different times and might not even be in the same room at the same time. It is often up to the studio engineer to shape the raw material to exact time requirements.

1 Click on the Import File button (🖹) and Ctrl-click the following files from the AA_07 folder:

• Announcer_1.wav

• Announcer_terms.wav

• Announcer_tincan.wav

• Announcer_welcome.wav

• SkyCellTell_theme.wav

• Woman1_thankyou.wav

• Woman1_cantbelieve.wav

2 Double-click on the Announcer_1.wav clip to load it into the Edit View. Press your spacebar to hear the clip, which is approximately 20 seconds long.

3   To ensure you are working in the correct time format of minutes and seconds, choose View > Display Time Format and select Decimal if it is not already chosen. This clip was read in one take, you will be splitting it to create two separate clips. Using the Time Selection tool (I), click and drag to select from the beginning of the clip to the 7.5 second mark.

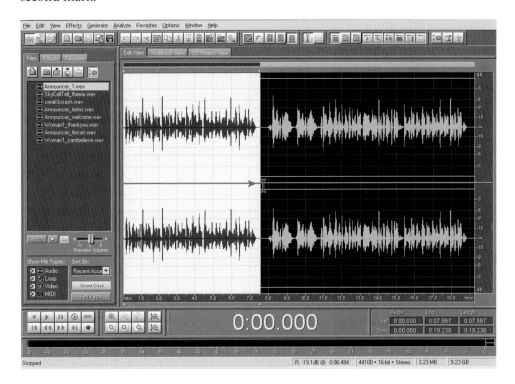

4   Choose Edit > Copy to New. The selection becomes its own waveform and appears in the display window. Choose File > Save As and save the file as **Announcer_intro.wav** into your AA_07 folder, located in the AA_CIB folder on your hard drive. If prompted to overwrite the file click Yes, then OK.

5   Double-click on the file Announcer_1.wav in the Organizer window. Notice that the first selection remains highlighted, which makes it easier to create a second selection.

6   Click on the waveform at the 8 second mark and drag to the right, selecting the second half of the waveform.

7 Press the Play button and note how the announcer repeats the first phrase "Well, it's true." To edit out the first instance of the phrase, shift-click on the timeline at the 9.5 second mark. This moves the first range boundary to the right and reduces the current selection by about 1.5 seconds.

Note: In addition to shift-clicking the timeline to adjust the range of the selection, you can also drag the range boundaries (represented as yellow triangles at the top and bottom of the timeline) to the left or to the right to expand or contract the selection.

Trimming and placing a clip

In the next steps you will start placing and trimming various clips to create the final session.

1 Choose Trim from the Edit menu, trimming a clip retains the selected area and deletes everything else.

2 Choose File > Save As and rename the file **Announcer_itstrue.wav** and save it into your AA_07 folder which is located in the AA_CIB folder on your hard drive.

3 You will now begin to place your files into the session. Click the Multitrack View tab and rename track 1 by highlighting the track name and entering **Announcer**. Repeat this process to rename track 2 to **Woman 1**, track 3 to **Sound Effects** and track 4 to **Music**.

4 Target the Announcer track by clicking on it. Click on the Announcer_intro.wav file in the Organizer window to select it and then press the Insert key on your keyboard (*Ins* on some keyboards) to insert the clip into your multitrack.

5 Click and drag the woman1_cantbelieve clip into the Woman 1 track. Select the Multitrack View button ( ) and move the clip so the beginning aligns with the end of the Announcer_intro.wav.

The edges of the two clips aligned because of a feature called Snapping. While this is helpful with music-based sessions, it is not always helpful with vocal projects where you may wish vocals to overlap slightly.

6 Choose Edit > Snapping and select both the Snap to Clips and the Snap to Loop Endpoints options to deselect them. Additionally, deselect the Snap to Ruler (Coarse) option so it is not checked. If the Snap to Ruler (Fine) option is checked, also deslect it and then position the woman1_cantbelieve.wav so the clip begins at 0:07.000.

Note: Audition measures time in the decimal format down to a thousandth of a second. We have rounded off all measurements in the text to tenths of a second, the actual numbers in your session may differ slightly.

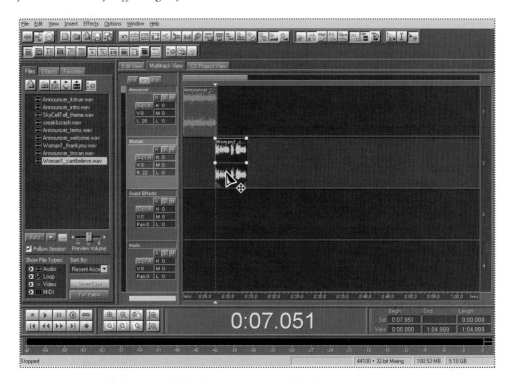

7   The current-time indicator is the bar with the yellow triangles at the top and bottom of the timeline. Click and drag the current-time indicator to 0:14.00 on the timeline. Drag the file Announcer_itstrue.wav into the Announcer track and align the beginning of the clip to the current-time indicator.

8   Move the current-time indicator to 0:23.900. Drag the file Announcer_tincan. wav into the announcer track and align the beginning of the clip to the current-time indicator.

9   Move the current-time indicator to 0:35.700. Place the clip Woman_thankyou. wav into the Woman1 track and align the beginning of the clip on the current-time indicator.

Note: If you run out of room to place the additional clips, you will need to click the Zoom Out Horizontally button (⊖) in order to view more of the timeline.

10 Move the current-time indicator to 0:50.200. Place the clip Announcer_welcome. wav into the Announcer track and align the beginning of the clip to the current-time indicator.

11 Place the Announcer_terms.wav into the Announcer track next to the Announcer_ welcome.wav at (1:01.00). Press the Home key to send the current-time indicator to the beginning of the session and press the spacebar on your keyboard to play. If you hear obvious gaps or overlaps between clips, adjust them now by selecting the Move/Copy Clip tool and dragging the clips to the left or the right.

12 Press the Home key to place the current-time indicator at the beginning of the timeline and then press the spacebar to begin playing the session. When the creaking chair sound effect stops at the 7 second mark, press the spacebar to stop playing the session.

Playing the creaking chair sound effect over the voice-over may have seemed like a good idea, but in practice the two tracks are competing with each other. You will move the other files to the right of the creaking chair effect.

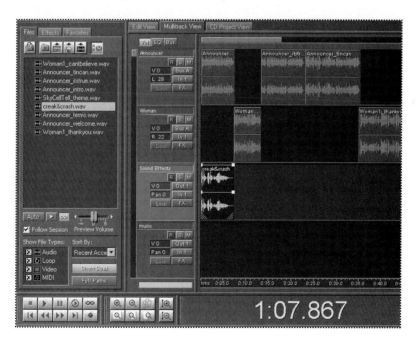

13 If necessary, choose the Multitrack View button (📑). Place your cursor in the lower right corner of track two. Click and drag up and to the left to create a marquee which selects all the tracks. All the clips in track 1 and 2 should be selected.

14 Click and drag the current-time indicator to the 4.1 second mark. This will be the point in the session in which the announcer begins speaking. You will overlap the Announcer_intro clip with the creaking chair sound effect. Click and drag all the selected clips to the left, making sure the beginning of the Announcer_intro clip is aligned with the current-time indicator.

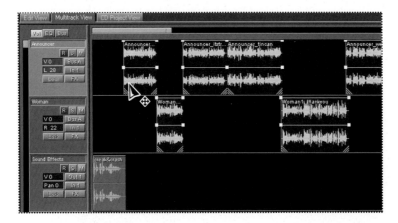

15 Click on the Zoom Out Full Both Axis button (🔍). In the lower right-hand corner in your Selection/View controls, note the overall length of the commercial is longer than one minute. Our session length is 1:15, your numbers may differ slightly. You will need to edit clips in order to shorten the overall session length and meet the time requirements of one minute.

16 Click and drag the current-time indicator to the beginning of the Announcer_ tincan clip. If you need help in identifying a clip name, place your cursor over the various clips in the timeline and the full name of the clip appears at the bottom of the display window. Press the spacebar and listen to the clip. When the clip is done, press the spacebar to stop playback.

17 Move the current-time indicator to the 37.5 second mark and press the spacebar to play from this point. You will be cutting the phrase "But don't take my word for it, listen to what Jennifer Smith of Fargo, North Dakota has to say." If the phrase is cut off or if there is part of the previous phrase, move the current-time indicator and press the spacebar again. Once you have located this phrase, click the Time Selection tool (I) and click and drag from the current-time indicator to the end of the clip.

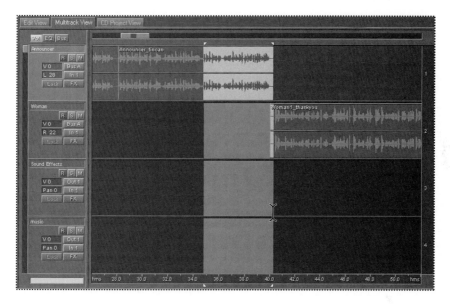

18 Choose Edit > Cut to remove this section from the multitrack.

19 Place your cursor at the beginning of the next clip, Woman1_thankyou.wav. Highlight the entire clip from beginning to end by clicking and dragging across the clip. Click the Zoom to Selection button ( ) to view the entire waveform in the display window.

20 Press the spacebar to listen to the clip. You will be deleting the phrase "I've gone though several cell phone companies and none of them lived up to my expectations." Place your current-time indicator at approximately the 47.5 second mark and press the spacebar. The phrase you want to keep is "Skycelltell has the best reception, best price, best customer service of any company I've ever known. Thank you Skycelltel!" You may need to move your current-time indicator and press the spacebar a few times until you are satisfied.

21 Once you have located the phrase, click the handle at the bottom left corner of the Woman1_thank you clip and drag it to the right until it aligns with the current-time indicator. This cuts the first phrase and shortens the clip.

💡 *When used with looped files, the handles on the bottom left and right of the clips repeat and extend music loops. On standard audio clips the handles are still useful. If you cut too much off the beginning or end of a clip you can drag the handles to restore portions of the original audio.*

22 Click the Zoom Out Full Axis button (🔍). Note there is a gap of approximately 10 seconds from the audio you deleted. Using the Move/Copy Clip tool, shift-click on the three clips Woman1_thankyou, Announcer_welcome and Announcer_terms and drag them to the left. Align the beginning of the clip Woman1_thankyou.wav with the end of clip Announcer_tincan.wav.

23 Press the Home key to return the current-time indicator to the beginning of the session. Press the Play button to listen to the entire commercial. If there are any obvious gaps between clips, use the Move/Copy Clip tool to adjust the position of clips as necessary.

Using the delete silence command

Removing the approximately 10 seconds of content from your commercial got you closer to the one minute mark, but the length of the session is still a few seconds too long. You will use Audition's capability of automatically deleting the silence between words and phrases.

1   Double-click on the clip Woman1_cantbelieve.wav in your Organizer window. This opens the file and displays the waveform in the Edit View. Press the spacebar to hear the clip. The actor's delivery includes a pause between words, visible as valleys in the waveform. The Delete Silence command automatically removes multiple areas of silence within a clip.

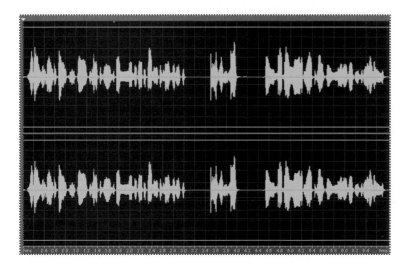

2   Choose Edit > Delete Silence and the Delete Silence window opens. In the Delete Silence window, click the Find Levels button. Audition scans the waveform for areas which it considers silence.

Applying the Delete Silence command analyzes and deletes silence across the entire waveform by default. You can also make a selection before choosing the command to impact only a specified portion of the waveform.

3   Click the Scan for Silence Now button. Audition previews the scanned area and gives you an approximation of how much silence will be deleted. For this waveform the results should be slightly more than one-quarter of one second (0.28). Click the OK button.

4   Press the Play button or use the spacebar on your keyboard to hear the edited clip. You should notice the phrase is shorter, but there are still gaps between the words. Press Ctrl + Z to undo the Delete Silence. You will modify the default settings to remove more of the gaps between the words.

5   Choose Edit > Delete Silence. Click the Find Levels button. In the "Silence" field change -64dB to -54dB. In the "Audio" field change –59.4dB to -49dB.

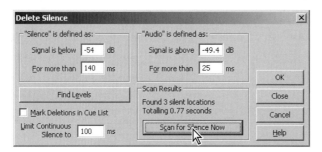

6   Click the Scan for Silence Now button. Audition will locate more silence as you broaden the definition it used when locating silent portions of the waveform. Using the values you entered in step 5, Audition should locate additional silent locations and remove approximately three-quarters of one second. We removed .77 seconds in 3 locations. Click OK and then click the Play button to hear the new waveform. There should be a very minimal pause between the words.

To better hear the difference between the two clips, press Ctrl + Z to undo the Delete Silence command and play the clip. Redo the Delete Silence by pressing Shift + Ctrl + Z. Listen carefully to the clip and make sure that none of the vocals have been cut. If you find that words or parts of words are being cut, you should undo the command and adjust the parameters for the audio and the silence levels. In general, if words or phrases are chopped off you should lower the signal level values. If not enough silence is removed, increase the signal level values.

7   Choose File > Save As. Enter the name **Woman1_cantbelieve(edited).wav**. Because the Delete Silence command is performed in the Edit View, the changes are destructive. By choosing Save As and renaming the file, you maintained a copy of your original audio in case you need it later.

8   Return to the Multitrack View and view the edited clip. Deleting silence from a clip has the desired effect of making the clip, shorter, however you will now need to adjust the subsequent clips to avoid gaps between the voices.

9   If necessary, choose the Multitrack View button ( ). Shift-click to select the five clips to the right of the Woman1_cantbelieve(edited) clip. Drag the clips to the left, aligning the start of the Announcer_itstrue.wav clip with the end of the Woman1_cantbelieve(edited)_incredible clip.

10   Click on the Zoom Out Full Both Axis button ( ). Note the overall length of the session in your Selection/View controls, the length should read approximately 1:01. Click on the last clip in the Announcer track, (Announcer_terms.wav) to select it. Click the Clip Time Stretching button ( ) in your toolbar. You will be using the time stretching feature of Audition to reduce the length of this clip from 5 seconds to 4 seconds.

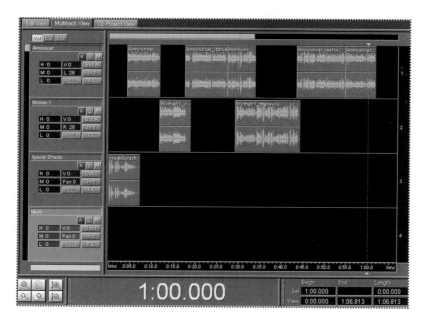

11 Move the current-time indicator to the 1 minute mark in the timeline. On the right side of the Announcer_terms clip, select the handle and drag until the end of the clip snaps to the current-time indicator.

Like other features in Multitrack View, time stretching is nondestructive, so you can disable it at any time.

What is Time Stretching?

Time stretching lets you change the length of an audio clip without changing its pitch. This technique is particularly helpful for fitting audio clips to video scenes or layering clips for sound design. You can time stretch a clip either by dragging or by setting time stretch properties. When you time stretch by dragging, Adobe Audition analyzes a clip's contents and attempts to select the most natural sounding time stretch method. When you set properties for time stretching, you also specify the method of time stretching to use.

Time stretching changes the tempo of a clip. If you time stretch a loop-enabled clip, it won't match the session tempo.

12 Press the Home key on your keyboard to return the Play cursor to the beginning of the session and then press the spacebar to review your edits to the commercial.

Using the bus mixer

The bus mixer is an efficient way to group tracks together to apply the same effects to both tracks. Here you will group the Announcer track and the Woman track together. Although you could add the same effect individually to the two tracks, grouping them together will save you time, especially if you decide you need to modify the effect.

1 If necessary, choose Window > Mixer to open the Mixer window. If the Mixer window is docked, grab it by the double handles and drag it to the center of the Multitrack View display area.

2   If you do not see the 4 tracks in the Mixer window, you will need to expand the window wide enough to see them. Place your cursor on the right-hand edge of the window until a double-arrow is displayed. Click and drag the window to the right, expanding the visible area so that all four tracks are displayed.

Expanded Mixer window.

3   Click on the Bus Mixer tab in the Mixers window and click on the New button in Bus A. The Bus Properties window opens.

4   In the field named Friendly Name enter **Studio Reverb**. Click on the plus sign next to Delay Effects and then click on the Studio Reverb effect.

5 Click on the Add button to place the Studio Reverb into your Current Effects Rack.

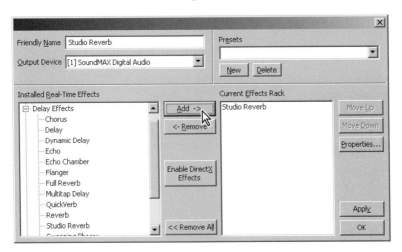

6 In the Current Effects Rack field, click on Studio Reverb and then click on Properties. The Studio Reverb window opens.

7 From the Preset menu in the Studio Reverb tab, select Room Ambience 1. Click the Close button to close the Studio Reverb window. Then click OK on the Bus window. Make sure your Mixer window is still open.

8 In the Announcer track, click on the button marked Out 1 ( ), located directly beneath the Record, Solo and Mute buttons. The button name changes to Bus A, signifying that the output of the Announcer track is passing through Bus A. Because Bus A has the Studio Reverb effect applied to it, all clips on the Announcer track will have the effect as well.

9 Press the Home key to return the current-time indicator to the beginning of the session, press the spacebar to begin playing. Note the difference between the Announcer's voice and the woman's voice. Only the Announcer track is affected by the Studio Reverb. The Studio Reverb effect adds various amounts of reverberation to a track, simulating the effect of a voice or musical instrument inside a specific room space. In this case, Room Ambience 1 places the Announcer's voice inside a small room.

10 If the session is still playing, press the spacebar to stop it. Click on the Out button ( ) on the Woman track to open the Playback Devices window. Click on Studio Reverb in the Busses field, then click the OK button. This adds the audio from the Woman track into the Studio Reverb bus. The same effect is now being applied to both the Announcer and the Woman 1 tracks.

A benefit of adding multiple tracks to a single bus is that changes made to the bus properties automatically change the properties across all tracks on the bus. You will hear this when you use the volume slider on the bus.

11 In the Mixer window, click on the Bus Mixer tab if it is not already chosen. The Bus Mixer controls allow you to change the properties of all tracks added to the bus. Press the spacebar to begin playing the session. Drag the volume slider down to -6 dB in the Studio Reverb bus. Both the Announcer and Woman tracks are affected by the change. Bring the volume slider back to 0 dB and press the spacebar to stop playing the session.

12 Click on the Track Mixer tab in the Mixers Window and then click on the Bus button. This adds a bus section with wet and dry values. The Wet value is the amount of the effect signal, by default this is set to 100. The Dry value is the amount of the Original signal, which is set to 0 by default.

Bus section displayed in Mixers window.

13 Change the Wet Value for the announcer to 80 by clicking and dragging towards the left, in the Wet value field. Change the Dry value to 20 by clicking and dragging in the dry value field. Close the Mixer window.

Adding effects and equalization

To add the finishing touches to your commercial, you will add an effect to the announcer's voice, add a music track, and then mixdown the file.

1 In the Organizer window double-click the clip Announcer_tincan.wav to open it in the Edit View.

2 Choose the Time Selection tool (I), then click the waveform and drag to the right to create a selection from the beginning of the clip to the 3.4 second mark. This selects the phrase "Most cell phones sound like you're talking through a tin can…" Be certain that you do not include the remaining part of the sentence: "…With Skycelltell it sounds like you're in the same room." If necessary you can adjust the selection by grabbing the yellow range marker and dragging it to the left or to the right.

3 Choose Effects > Filters > Quick Filter. The Quick Filter window opens.

4   In the Quick Filter window, click to select the Old Time Radio preset. Check the
Enable Preroll and Postroll Preview checkbox, if it is not already selected, and then click
the Preview button. You will hear the phrase you selected take on a higher, tinnier tone.
Because you have the Postroll Preview checked, you can also hear the first two seconds
of the unaltered audio after the end of the selection, allowing you to compare the effect
of the Old Time Radio filter. Press the Stop button to stop playing the selection.

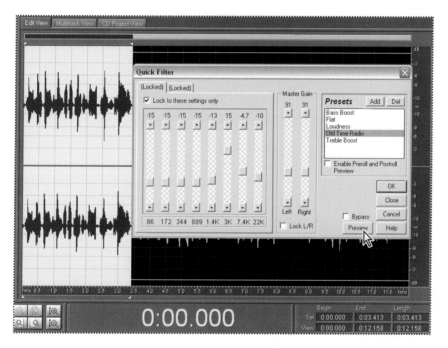

> ### The Quick Filter
>
> *The Quick Filter is an 8-band graphic equalizer that suits many filtering needs. Unlike a standard graphic equalizer, settings for the individual frequency bands interact with nearby frequencies. For example, significantly boosting the level of the highest 22 kHz frequency band moderately boosts the level of lower frequencies. This behavior helps to quickly and easily enhance audio tone.*
>
> —From Adobe Audition Help

5   In the settings for Master Gain, check to select the box for Lock L/R. Increasing the EQ frequencies often increases the volume of the waveform as well. Locking the Left and Right gain ensures that we are reducing the volume of the left and right channels equally.

6   Click the Preview button to hear the selection again. The clipping of the audio is noticeable as a crackling noise at the highest levels of the waveform. Grab the left slider and drag it down to a lower value, listen until you no longer hear the crackling noise. We used a value of 25. Click the OK button to commit the effect. Note the changes to the waveform.

7   Click on the Multitrack View tab. Press the Home key to return the current-time indicator to the beginning of the session and then move your current-time indicator 20 seconds into the session. Press the spacebar to play the session from the 20 second point forward.

Remember that effects made to a file in the Edit View are destructive, although the changes do not impact the file until it is saved. If you need to make a change to an effect, return to Edit View, undo the effect and apply it again using different settings.

8   Double click the Announcer_tincan.wav clip to return to the Edit View. Select File > Save As to open the Save As window. Enter a name for this file **Announcer_tincan_edited.wav**.

9   Move the current-time indicator to 2.2 seconds in the timeline. From the Organizer window, drag the audio file skycelltell_theme.wav into the track named Music. Align the beginning of the clip with the current-time indicator.

Note: If you do not have the skycelltell_theme clip in your Organizer window, you will need to import it from the AA_07 folder by choosing File > Import.

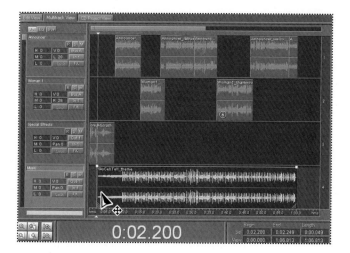

10   Press the Home key to return the play cursor to the beginning of the session. Press the spacebar to play the commercial. The music track was designed to be background music, but its sound levels are competing with the vocals. Press the spacebar to stop playing the session. Choose Window > Mixer to open the Mixer window.

11 In the Mixer window click, on the Bus Mixer tab. Press the spacebar to begin playing the session. In the mixer window for the Studio Reverb bus, move the volume slider up to 1 dB. This makes track 1 and 2 slightly louder because you connected them to a bus earlier in the lesson.

12 Click on the Track Mixer tab. Note the volume for each track is still at zero. If it is not already selected, click on the Pan button at the bottom of the track mixer.

13 Click on the Pan field for the Announcer track and drag to the left, setting a value of L 28. This places the Announcer's voice slightly to the left of center in the stereo field.

14 Click on the Pan field for the Woman track and drag to the right, setting a value of R 28. This places the Woman's voice slightly to the right in the stereo field. Placing the two voices in opposite directions in the stereo field creates depth and adds to the illusion of a conversation. Close the Mixer window by clicking the close button.

15 Select File > Save Session.

16 Now you will mix down from 4 tracks to 2 tracks. Choose Edit > Mix Down to File and choose the All Audio Clips submenu. If the Embed Project Link window appears, click the Yes button to accept. The Embed Project Link adds identifying information which will allow other Adobe programs such as Premiere Pro to link to this file.

17 A file named Mixdown appears in the edit view. Choose File > Save As from the menu and name this file **SkyCellTell_60secFinal.wav** and click OK.

18 You have now completed this lesson. Press the spacebar to preview the finished file.

Review questions

1   What is the Delete Silence command and when is it used?

2   Where is the Bus Mixer and what does it control?

3   When and how is the Track Mixer used?

Review answers

1   Delete Silence is found in the Edit menu of the Edit View. It is used to automatically delete areas of silence in an audio wave. It has the effect of speeding up your audio by reducing the pauses between words, but also has the effect of changing the pace of your audio. Too much deletion of silence can result in audio which sounds artificial and can even delete words or phrases if not used properly.

2   The Bus Mixer is a method of sending the signals of two or more audio tracks to another track. This allows you to add a single effect to multiple tracks. It can also be used to control the pan, or volume of multiple tracks with a single control. When multiple tracks are added to a bus with an effect, the amount of the effect can be increased or decreased for each track separately.

3   The Track Mixer is accessed via Window > Mixer. The Mixer can also be docked into the Audition interface. Although volume, pan and effects can also be controlled in the multitrack, controlling the tracks with the Mixer window is useful when you have multiple tracks.

On your own

1   Perform the Delete Silence on the remaining clips in the multitrack. The Announcer_itstrue.wav still has a silence between the first and second phrases.

2   Create a new bus by clicking on the Bus tab and then clicking the *Bus A* button in track 1. Add a new bus in the Playback Devices window and apply a different effect such as Chorus or Echo. Experiment with combining the two busses and layering the effects.

3   Using the Track Mixer, mix the session using different settings. Experiment with different levels for the two vocal tracks as well as the music track. Experiment with the pan levels.

Lesson 8

8 | Using the Bus Mixer and Real-Time Effects

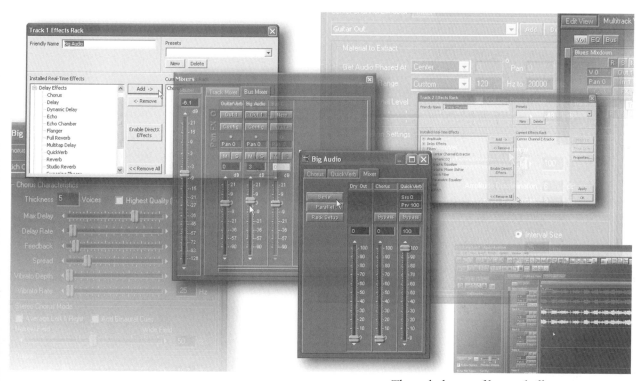

Through the use of bus and effects mixers, Audition provides a visual interface for added control. You can also conduct real-time effects processing using Audition's Multitrack View.

In this lesson, you will learn how to do the following:

• Use real-time effects.

• Use the bus mixer more efficiently.

• Use the Center Channel Effect to alter or remove a track.

Getting started

In this lesson, you will learn how to use Adobe Audition's real-time effects from the Multitrack View. This method allows you to adjust the type of effect and its details independent of the wave file or track. This type of effects processing is non-destructive because the effects processing occurs in the Multitrack, while destructive editing physically alters attributes of the waveform in the edit view. Multiple real-time effects can be used in combination on the same track. The effects can be re-ordered to alter the sonic texture of a file or saved as a preset and used elsewhere in the multitrack.

1   Start Adobe Audition and select the Multitrack View tab, if it is not already selected.

2   Choose File > Open Session, and open the 08_start.ses file in the AA_08 folder, which is located in the AA_CIB folder on your hard disk.

Note: If you have not already copied the resource files for this lesson onto your hard disk from the AA_08 folder from the Adobe Audition 1.5 Classroom in a Book *CD, do so now. See "Copying the Classroom in a Book files" on page 2.*

3   Choose File > Save Session As. Name the file **08_Effects.ses**, and save it in the AA_08 folder on your hard disk.

4   To play the finished session file, choose File > Open Session, and open the 08_end.ses file in the AA_08 folder, which is located within the AA_CIB folder on your hard disk. Play the session file by either clicking on the Play button () in the Transport Controls toolbar or pressing the spacebar on your keyboard.

5   When you are ready to start working, close the 08_end.ses file by choosing File > Close All, and reopen the 08_Effects.ses file you just saved by selecting File > Open Session.

Applying real-time effects

You will now use real-time effects on a track by accessing the Track Effects Rack option in Multitrack View. You will then save these settings as a preset to be used later, in another track in your multitrack session.

1   Click on the Track Effects Settings button of the Blues Mixdown track, currently labeled FX. The Track 1 Effects Rack window opens.

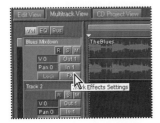

2   In the Track 1 Effects Rack window, enter **Big Audio**, in the upper left corner of the window as the new Friendly Name. This name replaces the Track Effects Settings button label of the multitrack.

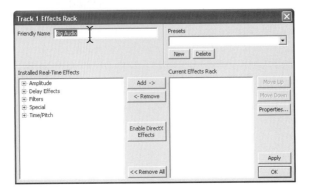

3   In the Installed Real-Time Effects portion of the window, click on the plus sign (⊞) beside the Delay-Effects option. This displays the available delay effects.

4   Click the Chorus option to select it, and then click the Add button, placing it in the Current Effects Rack.

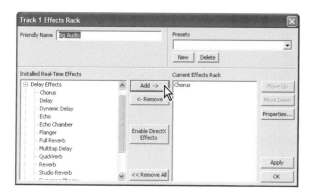

5   Click the QuickVerb Real-Time Effects option and then click the Add button, adding it to the Current Effects Rack as well.

6   Click the New button to create a preset, which also saves your changes. Enter the name **Big Audio** for the preset, then click OK.

7   Click the Properties button to open the Big Audio properties window.

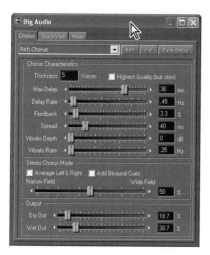

8   Press the spacebar to play your session file to hear the results of the real-time effects.

Although two windows are open (Track 1 Effects Rack window and Big Audio), you can still play the session file by pressing the spacebar on your keyboard or clicking the Play button (▶))

9   In the Big Audio window, confirm that the Chorus tab is selected. Choose the Rich Chorus option from the Presets menu. Press the spacebar to stop playback.

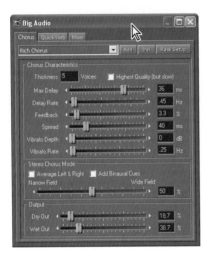

10 Click the Quick Verb tab from the Big Audio window. Choose the Ethereal preset from the menu, then press the spacebar or click the Play button to listen to your session with these effects applied. Press the spacebar once again to stop playback and continue.

11 Select the Mixer tab in the Big Audio window, revealing options for both the Chorus and Quick Verb effects.

Using the Mixer tab, you can change the ratio of Dry to Wet sound, bypass effects, and also combine effects as serial or parallel groups. Multiple effects are combined in serial groups by default. In serial groups, the signal travels directly from the output of one effect to the input of the next effect. In parallel groups, each effect receives the Dry signal independently. With parallel groups the effect outputs are mixed at equal levels equaling 100%.

💡 *You can adjust effect settings as the session plays, listening to the results in real-time.*

12 Click the Serial button in the Big Audio Mixer tab and press the spacebar to begin listening to the file. As the session file plays click the Parallel button to listen to your changes.

For serial groups, effect inputs are set to 0% of the Dry source, which is specified in the Src field, and the previous effect is specified at 100% in the Prv field. All effect output sliders are set to zero except for the final slider, which is set to 100%.

For parallel groups, effect inputs are set to 100% of the Dry source and 0% of the previous effect. With parallel groups, effect output sliders are set to an equal level. For example, if there are three effects, each is set to 33%, while if there are four effects, each of the effects is set to 25%.

Note: The first effect in the Big Audio Mixer tab lacks Src and Prv text boxes because no previous effect exists.

13 Click the Parallel button and close the window by clicking the close button in the upper right corner of the window.

14 In the Track 1 Effects Rack window, click OK to close the window.

15 Choose File > Save Session.

To bypass all real-time effects for a track, right-click the FX button in the track controls, and choose Bypass from the context menu.

Using the Center Channel Extractor Effect to alter or remove a track

The Center Channel Extractor Effect isolates frequencies that are equal in both the left and right channels. You can use this to isolate sounds that are panned center as opposed to the left or right channels. It is common to find voice, bass, and lead instruments recorded this way. As a result, you can use this effect to isolate the vocals, lead instrument, bass, or kick drum in order to amplify or remove them from the stereo mix.

You will apply the Center Channel Extractor effect to a second occurrence of TheBlues.wav file in your multitrack session to simulate the karaoke effect on the lead guitar track. You will also create an effect which increases the volume of the lead guitar, making it more prominent.

1 Right-click on the file labeled TheBlues.wav and choose Insert into Multitrack from the context menu. Audition places the file into Track 2 of the multitrack.

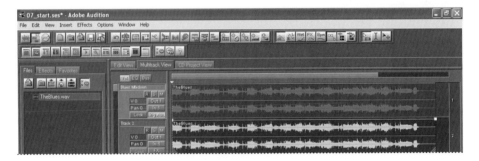

2 Click the Mute button () of the Blues Mixdown track, muting the playback of track 1.

3 Click the Track Effects Settings button () of Track 2. The Track 2 Effects Rack window opens.

4   Enter **Center Channel**, in the upper left-hand corner of the window as the new Friendly Name. This name replaces the Track Effects Settings button label of the multitrack.

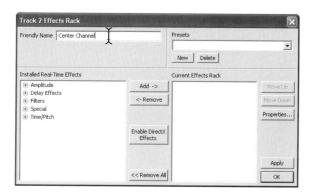

5   In the Installed Real-Time Effects portion of the window, click on the plus sign (⊞) adjacent to the Filters option.

6   Choose the Center Channel Extractor effect and click on the Add button. The Center Channel Extractor effect is added to the Current Effects Rack.

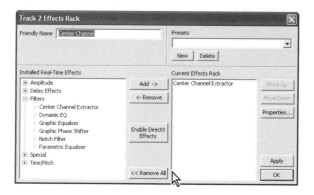

7   Click the Properties button, opening the Center Channel properties window.

8   In the Center Channel properties window, choose the Vocal Remove option from the drop-down list. Then press the spacebar to play the multitrack. The guitar frequency levels are reduced dramatically.

9   In the Center Channel properties window, click and drag the Center Channel Level slider to the left, changing the value to -48dB. Click and drag the Discrimination Settings slider to the right until its value is 100. Press the spacebar to stop playback, then press the Home key on your keyboard to reset the play cursor to the start of the loop. Then press the spacebar to play the loop and to listen to your changes. When you are finished press the spacebar once again to stop playing the file.

10   Click the Add button in the Center Channel properties window to save your changes as a preset. Enter **Guitar Out** as the new preset name, then click OK.

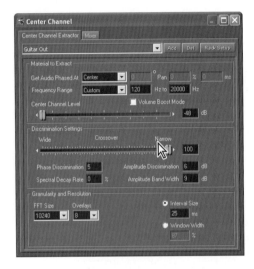

From the drop-down list in the Center Channel properties window, select the Amplify Vocals 6dB option. Press the spacebar to listen to your changes. When you are finished press the spacebar once again to stop playing the file. This option creates an inverse effect, amplifying the Guitar frequencies that were muted in the Guitar Out preset you created previously.

11   From the drop-down list in the Center Channel properties window, choose the Guitar Out preset. Close the window by clicking in the upper right corner of the window, then click OK to close the Track 2 Effects Rack Window.

12   Choose File > Save Session.

Advanced bus mixer usage

You will now use the real-time effects created earlier in this chapter on the original multitrack file, with the use of buses. Buses allow you to collectively output multiple tracks through an effect or group of effects as the track plays. This allows for more efficient computer process as opposed to duplicating the same effect on each individual track. You can use up to 26 buses per multitrack session file.

1 Select File > Append to Session. Navigate to the AA_08 folder on your hard disk and select the Blues.ses file, then click Open. The original multitrack session file opens and is appended to your current file. Five more tracks are added to your session file.

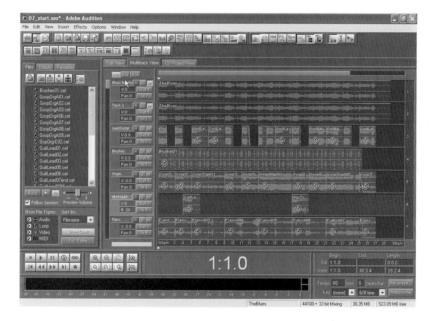

2 Mute Track 2 by clicking the Mute button ( ) in the Track Controls.

3 Click the Out 1 button ( ) in the Track Controls of the LeadGuitar track, opening the Playback Devices window.

4 In the Playback Devices window, click on the New Bus button. The Bus B Properties window opens.

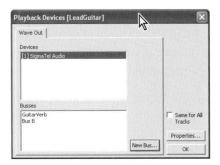

5 In the Bus B properties window, enter the new Friendly Name of **Big Audio Bus** in the upper left corner of the window.

6 In the Preset option, click on the drop-down and select the Big Audio preset. This is the preset you created earlier in the lesson. Click OK to close the window.

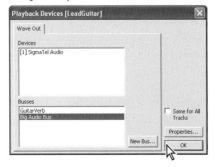

7 In the Playback Devices window, click to select the Same for all tracks option, located above the Properties button, then click OK. The Same for all tracks option applies the same output device, in this case the Big Audio Bus, to all the tracks in your multitrack session file.

8 Preview your file by pressing the spacebar on your keyboard or clicking the Play button in the Transport Controls. The effects of the selected bus are noticeable in the newly placed tracks.

9 Click the Output 1 button, currently labeled Bus B, of the LeadGuitar track. The Playback Devices window opens. In the Playback Devices window, select GuitarVerb in the Busses portion of the window, and then click the OK button.

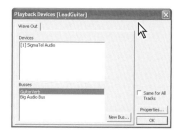

The Output Device button now reads Bus A, although the actual name of the bus is GuitarVerb.

10 Click the Output Device buttons of both the MoreLead and Piano tracks, individually changing the output device for each track to GuitarVerb. You should now have three tracks: LeadGuitar, MoreLead and Piano which are all using Bus A—the GuitarVerb bus.

11 Press the spacebar to play your session file. Choose File > Save Session.

12 Click on the Hide/Show Mixer toggle button ( ) to open the mixers window, then click the Bus Mixer tab.

13 Press the spacebar to play the session. Note that both busses are labeled accordingly.

14 Click and drag the volume slider of the Big Audio bus to 3dB. Note the slight adjustment while the file is playing.

15 When you are done listening to your file, press the spacebar to stop playback then close the Mixers window. Choose File > Save Session.

Review questions

1   Does the use of real-time effects work in a destructive or non-destructive manner?

2   How can you tell if a track is using a real-time effect?

3   How does the Center Channel Extractor Effect work?

Review answers

1   Real-time effects are non-destructive in nature, because the original file is being manipulated as a result of an effect during play, as opposed to the physical manipulation of the waveform itself via Edit View.

2   The Track Effects Settings button label will change to indicate the selected effect by name or by number.

3   The Center Channel Extractor Effect isolates common frequencies that occur in both the left and right channels equally—frequencies which are panned to center.

On your own

1   Open the Mixers window by clicking on the Hide/Show Mixers button (▥), then click on the Track Mixer tab.

2   Expand the window as necessary to view all seven of your current tracks by dragging the bottom right-hand corner of the window.

3   Note that the first two tracks are still listed as being Muted from the initial steps of this exercise. Click on the Out and Bus buttons in the bottom left-hand corner of the window to reveal output and bus options for each track.

4   Alter the Wet/Dry values for the GuitarLead track, pressing the spacebar to listen to your changes in real time. Note that you can also toggle between busses from the Mixers window by clicking on the Output Device button for each track.

5   After completing your changes choose File > Save Session.

9 | Using Audition's Equalization Tools

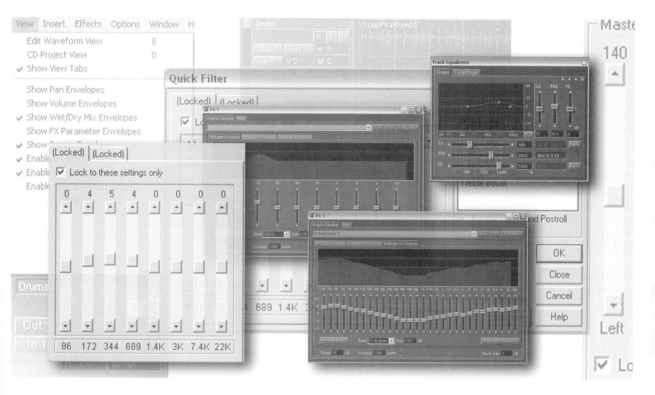

Audition provides a variety of methods for improving sound quality using Equalization techniques. Audition's Track Equalizers and Graphic Equalizer effect provide these controls. Additional control over Equalization levels is available using Wet/Dry Envelopes.

In this lesson, you'll learn how to do the following:

• Use the Quick Filter.

• Use Track Equalizers.

• Use the Graphic Equalizer effect.

• Work with Wet/Dry Envelopes and Equalization.

Getting started

Equalization is the art and science of emphasizing or reducing parts of the audio spectrum to produce a change in sonic texture. If you have ever adjusted the Bass and Treble control on a radio, you have used a very basic equalizer. More sophisticated equalizers allow you to precisely and selectively change the elements of a sound.

Note: Working with equalization requires very careful listening, as changes made to sounds can be quite subtle. Frequent work with equalization trains your ear to notice small changes in a sound. All the exercises in this chapter involve making changes to the frequency range of audio tracks. If you are using the built-in speaker on a laptop or other small computer speakers, the changes you apply may be less noticeable. If your computer speakers do not reproduce a wide range of sound, you may wish to use headphones for this lesson.

1   Start Adobe Audition. Click on the Multitrack View tab if not already selected.

Note: If you have not already copied the resource files for this lesson onto your hard disk from the AA_09 folder from the Adobe Audition 1.5 Classroom in a Book *CD, do so now. See "Copying the Classroom in a Book files" on page 2.*

2   To review the finished session file, choose File > Open Session... Navigate to the AA_CIB folder you copied to your hard disk, and open the file "AA09_end.ses" in the AA_09 folder. Click the Play to End button (▣) in the Transport Controls toolbar or press the spacebar on your keyboard. The completed file is played for you.

3   When you have finished listening to the file, close the 09_end.ses file by choosing File > Close Session and Its Media.

4   Choose File > Open Session and open the file "AA09_start.ses." You will start this exercise by modifying the equalization of an announcer's voice.

Using the Quick Filter

Audition's Quick Filter is an 8 band graphic equalizer that allows you to boost or cut the amplitude (volume) within a specific frequency range.

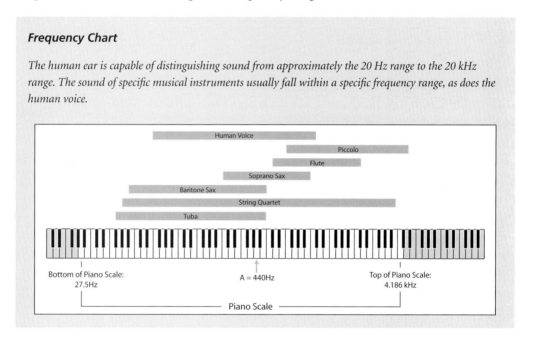

Frequency Chart

The human ear is capable of distinguishing sound from approximately the 20 Hz range to the 20 kHz range. The sound of specific musical instruments usually fall within a specific frequency range, as does the human voice.

1 In the Multitrack View, double-click on the announcer.wav clip to enter the Edit View. The Quick Filter effect is only available in Edit View.

2 Double-click on the center line, between the waveforms, to select the entire stereo waveform. Press the Play button (▶) to play the clip, which is 8.5 seconds in length.

3   Choose Effects > Filters > Quick Filter and the Quick Filter window opens. At the bottom of the Quick Filter window, the 8 bands span the range from 86 Hz, which is low end, or bass, to 22 kHz, which is high end, or treble.

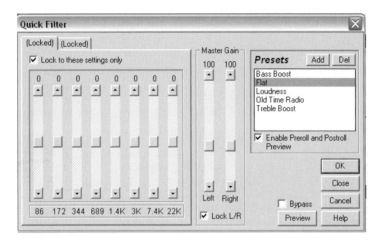

4   In the Quick Filter window, click the Preset name Flat to reset the amplitude values of all the frequency bands to 0. This removes the default values of the Quick Filter and allows you to modify each frequency band individually. You will make these modifications to better understand how each band impacts a vocal recording.

5   Click the Preview button to play the clip. As the voice is playing, click and drag the left-most frequency band slider, labeled 86, upwards. The value at the top of the slider changes as you push the slider up. This value represents the amplitude of this frequency.

This adjustment increases the volume of the low bass range of the announcer's voice. Push the slider up to the 14 value and you should hear the voice become deeper. Click on the Bypass check box to temporarily disable the effect and to hear the original audio. Click on the Bypass check box again to restore the effect.

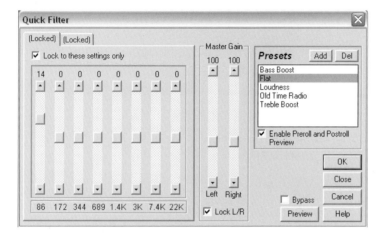

6   Press the Stop button to stop the preview of the effect. Click the Flat preset to reset the first slider, as you are going to try additional adjustments using the Quick Filter.

7   Click the Preview button to play the announcer clip. As the voice is playing, click and drag the right-most frequency band slider, labeled 22K, upwards. Change the amplitude value to 14.

This increases the treble and causes the voice to sound brighter. Listen to the phrase "Most cell phones sound…" and note that this adjustment to the high-frequency range accentuates the "s" sounds in this sentence. Exaggerated "s" sounds are referred to as sibilance. The more you increase the amplitude of high frequency levels the more likely you are to increase sibilance. Heavy sibilance sounds harsh and should be avoided. Decreasing high frequency levels often minimizes distracting sibilance.

8   Press the Stop button to stop the preview of the effect. Click the Flat preset to reset the adjustments you had made, as you will continue to experiment with equalization adjustments.

9 Click and drag the sliders for all 8 frequency bands individually upwards, changing all the amplitude values to 4.

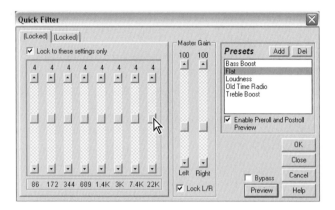

10 Click the Preview button. Increasing the amplitude values for all 8 bands equally raised the volume of the entire waveform. Click the Bypass checkbox in order to hear the original clip, which has a slightly lower volume level. Click the Bypass checkbox again to hear the effect of raising all 8 bands equally.

11 Click the OK button to apply the effect. The amplitude of the waveform increases. To compare the waveform before and after applying the effect, press Ctrl + Z to undo the Quick Filter. To reapply the effect press Ctrl + Shift + Z. Note the visual change in the waveform. Press Ctrl + Z one final time to undo the effect.

Using the Quick Filter to boost frequency bands may push amplitude levels above 0 dB, causing clipping, and therefore should be avoided. Changing the levels of all frequency bands is not an efficient way to adjust volume. Instead use the Amplify/Fade effect to increase or decrease volume levels.

12 Choose Edit > Repeat Last Command and the Quick Filter window opens. You can also use F2 as a keyboard shortcut to access this command.

13 Press the Flat preset to reset the sliders to zero. Move the slider for the 172 Hz frequency band to a level of 4. Increase the slider for the 344 Hz frequency band up to 5 and then push the slider for the 689 Hz frequency band up to 4. Click the Preview button to play the clip. Boosting the range between 172 and 689 Hz generally makes sounds warmer.

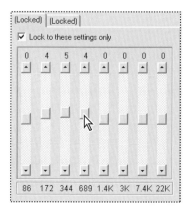

14 Click the Stop button to stop playing the clip. Click the Flat Preset to reset all the values. In addition to increasing frequency bands, you can also use the Quick Filter to reduce the frequency bands.

15 Click the Preview button to start playing the clip. Click and drag the 3K slider down until the amplitude value is -8. Then click and drag the 7.4 Hz slider down until its amplitude value is -9. Cutting the amplitude levels in the 3 to 7.4 kHz range reduces the higher frequencies, which emphasizes the lower frequency ranges. Because you reduced the amplitude levels you have a quieter overall waveform. This results in a warmer sound, similar to the sound achieved in step 13, although not as loud.

16 Click the Stop button to stop playing the clip. Click the Flat Preset to reset all the values, and then click on the Bass Boost preset. This preset changes the frequency bands and Master Gain values are set to 91. Master Gain is equivalent to the overall volume and it is set at a level of 100 by default.

17 If necessary, select the Lock L/R checkbox. Click and drag the master gain up to a level of 140 and then click the OK button. This increases the amplitude of the entire waveform, which makes the clip louder.

18 Choose File > Save As. Navigate to the AA_09 folder on your hard disk and enter the name **announcer_bass.wav** for this file. Remember that all edits you make in the Edit View are destructive, and if you want to keep both an edited and original version of the audio, you need to rename the edited file when saving.

19 Click on the Multitrack View tab to change to the multitrack. Choose File > Save As and rename this session **09_bassboost.ses** and save into the AA_08 folder on your hard disk.

Using Equalization in the Multitrack

Using the Quick Filter in the Edit View is a good way to quickly modify the tone of an audio clip. However, the Quick Filter uses destructive editing and it is applied one single clip at a time. If you want to apply equalization effects to all the clips in an entire track you must do so in the Multitrack View, using the equalization track controls.

1 Choose File > Open Session. Navigate to the AA_09 folder on your hard disk and click to select the multitrack_eq.ses file, and then click the OK button. This 4 track session file opens. Press the spacebar on your keyboard to play the session. When the session ends, press the spacebar to stop playing, and then press the Home key to return the current-time indicator to the beginning of the timeline.

2   Click the EQ tab at the top of the window in the track controls. This switches the track properties to EQ view.

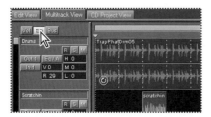

3   Click on the yellow S button (🟡S) in the Drums track to solo this track. Press the Play Looped button (∞) to begin playing the session.

4   There are three fields beneath the solo button marked H, M, and L. These represent the High, Middle and Low frequency bandwidths, respectively. Place your cursor over the field labeled M. This field controls the middle frequency values of the drum track, and the value is currently zero. Click and drag to the right, increasing the value to 6. This boosts the middle frequencies of the drum track by 6 db. The middle frequency corresponds to the bandwidth of the snare drum. Boosting this frequency creates a more pronounced sound for the drum track. Press the spacebar to stop playing the session.

5   Press the spacebar to start playing the session from the beginning. To compare the original EQ settings with the new EQ settings click the button labeled Eq/ A. The button label changes to Eq/ B and the Equalization Values are all set to zero, the default values for the track. Click on the Eq/ B button to switch back to the first EQ setting. The value for the middle EQ value remains where you set it, at the 6db level. Switching between the Eq/ A and Eq/ B banks provides an excellent way to compare EQ values and preview EQ changes in real-time.

6   Press the spacebar to stop playing the session. Next you will change the EQ values in the bass track. Select the Time Selection tool (I) then click and drag over the two clips, ClavBas03 and ClavBas02 starting at 3 bars 1 beat mark. Continue to drag to the 9 bar 1 beat mark, creating a selection that covers this range.

7   Click the yellow S button (![S]) in the Bass track to solo this track. Click the Play Looped button (![∞]) to only play the selection. Playing a looped selection allows you to focus on changing the EQ values without having to reset the current-time indicator each time the clip ends.

8   Place the cursor over the L text box. This field controls the Low frequency values of the bass track, and the value is currently set to zero. Click and drag to the right, raising the value to 8. This boosts the low frequencies of the bass track, which correspond to the lower bass values, by 8 db. Boosting this frequency creates a fuller sound for the bass guitar.

Note: Be cautious about boosting the lower frequencies of instruments such as bass guitars, bass drums or any electronic bass. Boosting the low frequency of a bass instrument may sound acceptable when using headphones or computer speakers, but the same effect may overwhelm the rest of the song when using a home or car stereo system. If you anticipate that audio will be played on a variety of devices, it is best to preview the audio using these different speaker systems before committing to a final mix.

9   Click the Eq/ A button to switch to the Eq/ B bank. The original values create a less pronounced bass track. Click the Eq/ B button to return to the Eq/ A bank. Press the spacebar to stop playing the ClavBas selection.

10   Choose File > Save to save your session.

Using the Track Equalizer window in the Multitrack

As you work on multitrack sessions with multiple instruments, you may need more precise control over frequency bandwith adjustments than the three equalizers in the Track Controls provide. Audition's Track Equalizer provides this control.

1   If necessary, choose the Time Selection tool (I). Click and drag over the entire B3LeslieLead clip located in the Leslie Organ track. The track is now selected.

2   Click the yellow S button (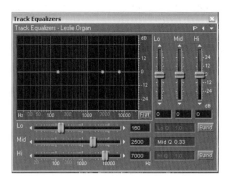) in the Leslie Organ track to solo this track. Right-click on the H field in the Leslie Organ track and the Track Equalizer window opens.

💡 *Right-clicking on any of the H, M or L fields opens the Track Equalizer window.*

3   Press the spacebar to play the Leslie Organ sample. To the right of the graph are three sliders marked Lo, Mid and High. Click and drag the Mid slider toward the top, boosting the midrange value to 7.5 dB. As you push the slider, the white anchor point on the equalization curve moves up the graph, and the line becomes curved, increasing the midrange results in a brighter and louder organ tone. Press the spacebar to stop playing the Leslie Organ.This method of changing the EQ values provides a visual graph of the amplitude change.

4   Press the spacebar to begin playing the Leslie organ sample. As the sample is playing, click and drag the Mid slider, located below the graph, to the left. Change its value from 2500 to 1000. The entire curve shifts to the left as you redefine the midtone frequency. This produces a different tone in the organ sample.

5   In the upper right corner of the Track Equalizers window, click the letter P. The EQ Preset window opens. Click the Add New button, then enter the name **Leslie Eq** and click the OK button. Saving the EQ Presets makes it easy to use the same adjustments on clips of similar style.

6   If necessary, click the downfacing white arrow on the far right side of the Track Equalizer and the Leslie track collapses into a tab. With the Track Equalizers window still open, click the drum clip and the EQ settings for the drum track are displayed in a new tab. Opening multiple tabs in the Track Equalizer window allows you to quickly switch between tracks and modify EQ settings.

7   Close the Track Equalizers window by clicking on the close button in the upper right corner. Choose File > Save Session to save your session. Then choose File > Close All to close the session and its associated media.

Using the Graphic Equalizer on a Final Mix

The Track Equalizers are excellent tools for changing the tonal qualities of individual instruments or groups of instruments. Once you have achieved a general balance with the Track Equalizers and have mixed down a session into a single waveform, you can apply the finishing touches using the Graphic Equalizer. In this exercise you will modify the equalization of a track. Other changes, such as volume and pan settings, along with effects, have already been applied to the file.

1   Choose File > Open Session. If necessary, navigate to the AA_09 folder and select the graphic_equalizer.ses file and click the Open button.

2   Press the Home key to position the current-time indicator at the start of the timeline. Choose the Time Selection tool (I) and then click and drag over the entire disco_eq clip to select it. Press the spacebar to play the disco_eq clip. This clip is a mixed down version of a song with a number of different instruments, including drums, guitars, bass and strings. There has been no equalization applied to the original tracks. When the clip is finished, press the spacebar to stop playback.

3   Click on the FX button (FX) to open the Track 1 Effects rack. Click the plus sign next to the Filters submenu, then click on the Graphic Equalizer effect. Click the Add button to add the Graphic Equalizer to the Current Effects rack, then click OK.

4   Click the FX 1 button in track 1. If you do not see the FX button, click the Vol tab in the track controls and click on the FX button. The FX 1 window opens, displaying the Graphic Equalizer controls. Click on the 10 Bands (1 octave) tab if it is not already selected. The Graphic Equalizer is similar to the Track Equalizer used in the previous exercise. Both equalizers provide control for boosting or cutting specific frequency bands, along with a visual representation of the process.

5 Click on the Reset All to Zero button to reset all the bandwidth levels to zero. The first slider controls the frequencies at 31 Hz and below while the last slider controls the frequencies above 16 kHz.

6 Press the spacebar to play the session. Click and drag the 125 Hz slider upwards to approximately 6 dB. As you move the slider, the Gain values change. Gain is represented in decibels, increasing the gain increases the volume of the frequency band. The 125 Hz range represents the low end, or bass range, of the frequency spectrum and you should hear a corresponding boost in the bass guitar. Press the spacebar to stop playing the song.

7 Click the tab marked 20 bands (1/2 Octave). This tab provides more precise control for adjustments to the frequency bands. The original 125 Hz range is now split into sliders for 88 Hz, 125 Hz and 180 Hz.

8 Click the tab marked 30 bands (1/3 Octave). This provides control beyond the 20 bands. The original 125 Hz range is now split into sliders for 80 Hz, 100 Hz, 125 Hz, 160 Hz and 250 Hz. Having access to more frequency bands results in finer control of the frequency values.

9   Click the small black arrow directly next to the Add button. This opens a drop-down menu, displaying a list of equalizer presets. Press the spacebar to play the session, and then choose the 30-band Classic V preset. You may have to scroll up to locate this preset.

Applying the preset changes the sliders to pre-determined values: the gain levels between 200 Hz and 3.2 kHz are cut, and the gain levels at the low and high ends of the frequency spectrum are boosted. This results in a sound that emphasizes the crisp, highhat cymbals as well as the electric bass. Classic V refers to the "V" shape this configuration creates with the sliders. These equalizer settings are used in the music industry to emphasize the bass and treble ranges of a song.

Note: Because every song is different, presets work best when used as the starting point for additional adjustments. For example, the Classic V equalizer preset could make an instrumental song sound brighter while the same preset applied to a vocal track may create a dull-sounding voice.

10   Press the spacebar to stop playing the session, then close the FX 1 window. Choose File > Save Session to save the current session. Keep the current session open for the next exercise.

Using the Track Envelopes to modify EQ levels

Because Equalization controls are real-time effects, they are applied non-destructively. The amount of each effect is controlled using track envelopes.

1   If necessary, click the FX 1 button in track 1 to open it. Press the spacebar to play the session. In the FX 1 window, click the preset menu and choose lo-fidelity. This dramatically changes the EQ levels by completely cutting the low and high frequencies, and results in a sound similar to what you might hear on an AM radio. Click on the Close button in the FX 1 window.

2   Click the View menu and confirm that Show Wet/Dry Mix Envelopes and Enable Envelope Editing options are selected. Also confirm that Show Volume Envelopes is not selected. The Volume Envelopes and the Wet/Dry Mix Envelopes both appear at the top of clips, having them both turned on can be confusing.

3   Press the spacebar to play four or five seconds of the clip to get a sense of the lo-fidelity EQ effect. Press the spacebar again to stop playing the session.

4   Place the cursor in the top left corner of the clip and click and drag the anchor point for the Wet/Dry Edit Envelope to the very bottom of the clip. A diagonal line stretches from the bottom left corner up to the top right corner of the clip. This applies none of the low-fidelity effect at the start of the clip and 100% of the low-fidelity effect at the end of the clip.

5   Press the spacebar to play the song. The music starts with the default EQ values. As the song progresses the low fidelity effect gradually increases until the effect is fully applied at the end of the song. Using the Wet/Dry Edit Envelopes allows you to modify the level of an EQ effect throughout a song. You can also apply different EQ settings throughout a song, as quiet sections of a classical song may require different values than those needed for a busy finale.

6   Choose File > Save Session and then choose File > Close All to close the session and its associated media.

Review questions

1   What is the definition of equalization and when is it used?

2   What is the Quick Filter and what are the advantages and concerns of using it?

3   What are Track Equalizers and when are they used?

Review answers

1   Equalization is the process of emphasizing or de-emphasizing parts of the audio spectrum. Equalization is used to change the harmonic structure of a sound or a musical instrument. Equalization can be used to make the bass line of a dance song more prominent or a soloist's voice in a chorus recital more present.

2   The Quick Filter is an 8 band graphic equalizer effect that is applied using the Edit View. It offers a simple interface that allows you to quickly change, and experiment with, the frequency levels of a sound. It must be used cautiously, as changes made to one frequency band will affect nearby frequency bands. Additionally, the Quick Filter is a destructive effect used in the Edit View so the effect is applied to only one clip at a time.

3   Track Equalizers are equalization controls which are enabled by default on every track in the Multitrack View. The Track Equalizers are separated into High, Middle and Low frequency ranges. They can be modified by clicking and dragging to raise or lower decibel levels. More precise control over frequency levels is accessed by right-clicking on any track equalization text box, which opens the Track Equalizers window. The Track Equalizers window offers enhanced control over equalization values.

On your own

1   Open the file announcer.wav used in the first exercise and open it into Edit View. Apply the Quick Filter effect and preview the different presets. If you have access to both headphones and a speaker system, compare and contrast the sound of the equalization effects when played through the different monitors.

2   Open the multitrack_eq.ses file used in the second exercise and Save As **multitrack_eq_onyourown.ses**. Use the Track Equalizer controls to make a track which emphasizes the low frequency or bass levels of the song. Save the resulting song by choosing File > Export > Audio. Return to the original session, and using the Track Equalizer controls, now make a track which emphasizes the high frequency or treble levels of the song. Export this track as well and compare the two. The process of Equalization often involves making several versions of the same song and evaluating the benefits of one mix over another.

3   Open the graphic_equalizer.ses file from the AA_09 folder on your hard disk and apply the graphic equalizer effect. Click on the 30-band view and experiment with the various sliders, identifying the frequency bandwidths for the string section of the song. Once you identify those frequencies, note how raising and lowering these frequencies affects the sound of other instruments in the song.

10 | Batch Processing and Scripting

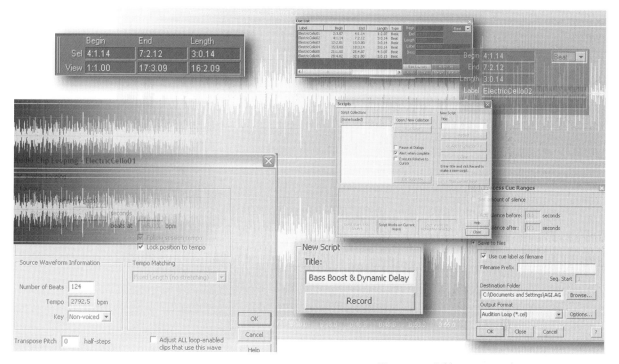

You can quickly create and export multiple looped music files using Audition's cue ranges and batch processing features. You can also work more efficiently with multiple files by taking advantage of Audition's scripting functionality.

In this lesson, you'll learn how to do the following:

• Use cues and batch processing to create individual loops.

• Use scripting to apply common effects to multiple files.

Getting started

1   Start Adobe Audition. Click on the Edit View tab.

Note: If you have not already copied the resource files for this lesson onto your hard disk from the AA_10 folder on the Adobe Audition 1.5 Classroom in a Book *CD, do so now. See "Copying the Classroom in a Book files" on page 2.*

2   To review the finished file, choose File > Open. Navigate to the AA_CIB folder you copied to your hard disk, and open the file "electric_cello_source_end.wav" in the AA_10 folder. If necessary change the Files of Type option to indicate ALL in the drop down menu of the Open window. Double-click electric_cello_source_end in your Organizer window to open it in Edit View. There are a series of six cue ranges marking six different sections of the waveform. The beginning of a cue range is visually identified by a red triangle and dotted line, the end of the cue range is visually identified by a blue triangle and dotted line. Each cue range represents an individual loop which will then be exported via Audition's Batch Export. The creation of cue ranges was first covered in Lesson 5, Working with Loops and Waves, although you will be creating them here as well.

3   Close the file by choosing File > Close All.

Defining Cue Ranges for Batch Export

In this exercise you will be adding cue ranges to a minute-long .wav file. This track was created by a musician playing an electric cello to the time of a drum loop. You will be defining the cue ranges for six sections of this performance and exporting each range as an individual cel file suitable for looping. This section will introduce you to the features of Audition's Batch Processing as well as the process for selecting bars and beats for looped files.

1   Open the file Electric_Cello_source.wav by choosing File > Open, and navigating to your AA_10 folder. Click the Open button to import the file into your Organizer window.

This file includes 8 cues, representing 4 cue ranges. You will be adding 2 more cue ranges in this exercise.

2   Press the spacebar to play the audio file, which is approximately 1 minute in length.

3   Choose Window > Cue List. The Cue List window opens and the 4 pre-defined cue ranges are displayed: ElectricCello01, ElectricCello02, ElectricCello03 and ElectricCello04. These cue ranges were added to the file for the purpose of this exercise.

4   Click and drag the Cue List window to the top of the Audition application window, placing your cursor directly above the Edit View tab. Release the Cue List window and it docks directly beneath the toolbars.

Cue List window docked into the Adobe Audition interface.

5   In the Edit View window, right-click on the timeline, which looks like a ruler along the bottom of the display, and choose Display Time Format from the context menu. A sub-menu appears. Confirm that Bars and Beats is highlighted. If it is not, select it now. You will be selecting full bars in order to create seamless loops.

6   Double-click the first cue range, ElectricCello01, in the Cue List window. The range between 2 bars 3 beats and 4 bars 1 beat is selected.

7   Press the Play Looped button (∞) to hear the selection. Listen to the loop two or three times and then press the spacebar on your keyboard to stop playing the selection.

8   In the Cue List window, double-click to select the cue range ElectricCello02. Note that the first cue range is deselected. Cue ranges are specific regions of a waveform that are saved as part of the file and can be accessed at any point. Press the AutoPlay button in the Cue List window and the second cue range begins to play.

9   Click on the third cue, ElectricCello03, to hear the cue range play. Because you selected AutoPlay in the last step, the cue range plays automatically.

10 Select the fourth cue, Electric Cello04, to hear the cue range play. Press the spacebar to stop playing the cue range.

11 Press the Home key to return the current-time indicator to the beginning of the timeline. You will now add two more cues to the cue list. If necessary, click the Zoom Out Full Both Axis button ( ) to display the entire waveform. Drag the current-time indicator to 3 bars 1 beat. You will be using the current-time indicator as a guide to create the beginning of your next selection.

12 Using the current-time indicator as a guide, place your cursor at the 3 bars 1 beat mark and then click and drag to the right, extending the selection to the 5 bars 2 beat mark (5:2.00). The selection starts at approximately 3 bars 1 beat and ends at approximately 5 bars 2 beats.

Note: Your numbers may be slightly different. Remember that Audition measures time in milliseconds, therefore matching our numbers exactly may be difficult.

13 Press the Play Looped button ( ) in the transport controls to hear the selected loop. After listening to the loop twice, press the spacebar to stop playing the selection.

14 Click the Add button in the Cue List window and this selection is added as a cue range in addition to the first four cue ranges in the Cue List. Note that all the cue ranges have the following properties: Label, Begin point, End point, Length, Type and Description. The Begin and End point as well as the length of the cue range are defined by the selection you made. The Label property for this new cue is Cue 03, a generic label name.

15 Click on the Edit Cue Info button if it is not already selected. A tab opens within the Cue List Window. Highlight the Label field and type **ElectricCello05**, and then press the Enter key to commit the change. This labels the cue range.

16 In the Edit Cue Info window, click the drop-down menu next to the Begin field. Change the cue type from Basic to Beat. Basic cues are markers between points on a waveform and could be used to identify a section of a speech. Beat cues are specifically used to mark musical beats. The definitions of types of cues are covered in Lesson 4, Working with Loops and Waves. You can also refer to the Adobe Audition Help for additional information.

17 Place your cursor at the 12 bars 2 beats mark (12:2.01), then click and drag to the 15 bar 3 beat mark (15:3.00). This creates a selection of 3 bars.

18 Click the Add button in the Cue List window and the selected cue range is placed in the Cue List. Click and drag in the Label field to select the text Cue 04 in the Edit Cue Info window and enter **ElectricCello06**. Click the drop-down menu and change the cue type from Basic to Beat. All 6 cue ranges are now defined and labeled.

19 Select File > Save As and rename this file **Electric_Cello_final.wav**. The sound wave now has 6 cue ranges which you have defined. Click on the word Label in the Cue List window. This will sort the cue ranges by name and rearrange them from 1 to 6. Before you can use the ranges effectively, you must convert them to individual files. You will do this using Audition's Batch command.

Batch processing cues

Selecting cues and cue ranges is the process of defining areas of a waveform that you want to use. For example, you may have recorded a long speech and wish to quickly identify sections of the speech. Once you have identified the important sections with cue ranges, Audition will allow you to automatically export each cue range as an individual file using its Batch command.

1   Click the Auto Play button in the Cue List window to turn off this function. Click on the ElectricCello01 cue range and then shift-click on the ElectricCello06 cue range in order to select all the cue ranges between. You are selecting the cue ranges in order to extract each range from the original waveform and save them as individual files.

2   Click the Batch button at the bottom of the Cue List window to open the Batch Process Cue Ranges window.

3   In the Batch Process Cue Ranges window, select the Save to files option. Confirm that the Use cue label as filename option is checked, then click on the Browse button next to the Destination Folder field. Navigate to the AA10 folder on your hard disk and select the folder named Batch_Process_Ouput then click OK. This folder was included with the lesson files.

4   While still in the Batch Process Cue Ranges window, click on the Output Format drop-down menu. The list of file formats that Audition is capable of exporting is displayed. If Audition Loop (*.cel) is not selected, choose it now. Click OK. Audition exports each cue range as a single file and saves it into the Batch_Process_Output folder that you specified.

Note: Because you are converting from a .wav file which is uncompressed to a cel file which is compressed, Audition may display a window indicating that you are saving to a lower fidelity file format. The default compression for Audition cel files is 320 kbs, which is very high quality. Click the option Don't display this message in the future and then click OK. Because this window can be suppressed by clicking the Don't display this message in the future option, it may not display when you save the file.

5   Click on the Multitrack View button (![icon]) to enter the Multitrack View. You will now import the 6 files into Audition to confirm the files exported correctly.

6   Move your cursor over an empty area of the Organizer window and double-click to open the Import window. Navigate to the AA10 folder on your hard disk to the Batch_Process_Output folder. The 6 ElectricCello cel files should be listed in this folder.

Note: If you don't see the files, make certain the Files of Type drop-down menu is displaying All Supported Media.

7   To select all the files in this folder, click on the ElectricCello1.cel file, then shift-click on the ElectricCello6.cel file. Click Open to import all the selected files into your session.

8   In the Organizer window, click to select the ElectricCello01 file and then click the Insert into Multitrack button (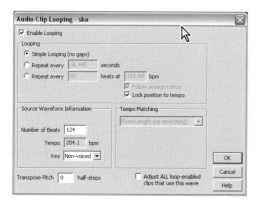). If necessary, click on the Multitrack View tab to enter the Multitrack View. Place your cursor on the bottom right corner of this clip and try dragging to the right to extend it. You cannot extend the loop because it does not have looping enabled.

9   Right-click on the ElectricCello01 file in the multitrack. From the context menu, choose Loop Properties. In the Loop Properties window, select the Enable Looping option, and then click OK.

10   Click and drag the bottom corner of the ElectricCello01 clip to extend the clip to the 4 bar mark. Press the spacebar to play the session, and at the end of the clip press the spacebar to stop playback.

11   Choose File > Save Session As... and name this session **AA10_batch.ses**. Make sure you are saving into your AA10 folder and click OK to save your session.

Creating and running scripts

Working with digital audio often involves working with multiple files of similar nature. Applying an effect such as Reverb to a single file does not take very much time, while applying the same effect to 50 individual files is a time-consuming process. Audition's Scripting capability allows you to apply effects to many files in a few easy steps. You will be using the files created from the previous exercise and applying different effects to these files.

1 If the previous session AA10_batch.ses is not already open, open it now.

2 Double-click on the file ElectricCello01.cel in order to open it in Edit View. Scripting can only occur in the Edit View.

3 Choose Options > Scripts. The Scripts window opens. We will be applying an effect to this window and using it as a template to apply to the other 5 files.

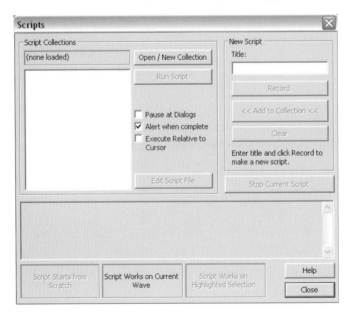

Scripts in Adobe Audition

Adobe Audition lets you create three types of scripts, depending on the software's state when you record the script:

- *Scripts that start from scratch. These scripts start with no waveform opened, and their first command is File > New.*

- *Scripts that work on the currently open waveform. These scripts operate on an entire waveform. They require a waveform to be open, but with no selection made. Actions begin at the current-time indicator position in the waveform, and they affect any data present at that point.*

- *Scripts that work on a selection. These scripts require a selection to be made first. Actions in the script apply only to the selection.*

—From Adobe Audition Help

4   In the Scripts window, click the Open/New Collection button. A window opens asking you to Choose a new Script file or enter a new name. The default Scripts folder, which is a subfolder in the main Audition 1.5 folder, is displayed, revealing the default scripts that are included with Audition. If the Scripts folder is not displayed, navigate through your hard drive to the Scripts subfolder located within the Audition 1.5 folder.

Note: A Script collection may include either one script or a number of different scripts.

5   Enter **myCIBscripts.scp** in the File name field and click Open. This saves your new script collection into the default Scripts folder. A script collection file uses the file extension of .scp.

6   In the New Script section of the Scripts window, enter the name **Bass Boost & Dynamic Delay** in the Title field, and then press the Record button. When recording, any effects you apply to the waveform are monitored and saved, so they can be applied to other files in the future. The recording only keeps track of the options selected, not the time it takes to select the options.

7   Choose Effects > Delay Effects > Dynamic Delay. The Dynamic Delay window opens. Choose Spacey from the list of presets. Press the Preview button to hear the effect of the Dynamic Delay. Click OK when done previewing. Dynamic Delay changes the amount of delay over the length of a waveform.

8   Choose Effects > Filters > Graphic Equalizer. The Graphic Equalizer effect boosts or cuts specific frequency bands and provides a visual representation of the resulting EQ curve. In the bottom left corner of the Graphic Equalizer window, choose the Simple Bass Lift preset. This preset primarily boosts the lowest frequencies and is similar to turning up the bass on a stereo system. Click the Preview button to hear the bass lift. Click the bypass option to hear the difference between the two settings. Click OK after previewing the edited clip.

9   Choose Options > Scripts to reopen the Scripts window. Click the Stop Current Script button to stop recording. Keep the Scripts window open.

Note: Had you applied additional effects to the waveform, the Script would have continued to record the additional effects.

10 In the blank text field at the bottom of the window enter **Added Dynamic Delay and boosted Bass. Works well on Electric Cello files** as a reminder for the next time you use this script.

11 Click the Add to Collection button and the Bass Boost & Delay loads into the Script Collection window on the left side of the application window. Note the description field is now locked. Anyone using this script will now see this description. Additionally, this provides a helpful reminder of which effects are used and in what order they are applied.

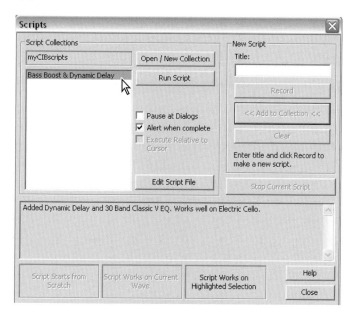

12 Click the Close button. You will now run this script on another file.

13 In the Organizer window double-click the ElectricCello02.cel to view the waveform. If you do not have the files ElectroCello02 through ElectroCello06 in your Organizer window, you may have previously closed your session and will need to import these files. Click the Import File button (🖼) located in the Files tab and shift-click ElectroCello2 and ElectroCEllo06 to import them.

14 Choose Options > Scripts from the menu. Click on the Bass Boost & Dynamic Delay script and click the Run Script button. The two effects are applied automatically and a confirmation window appears when the script is complete. Click the OK button to close the window.

You can run scripts on individual files, or you can run scripts on a number of individual files, which you will do later in this lesson.

15 Press the spacebar on your keyboard to play the clip. The same effects added to the ElectroCello01 clip have automatically been added to this clip.

16 Double-click on ElectricCello01.cel. Choose File > Save As and navigate to the Batch_Process_Output folder in you AA10 folder. Click on the New Folder button ( ) and name this folder ElectricCello_Space. Name the file you are saving **ElectricCello01_ Space.cel** and open the folder you just created inside the Batch_Process_Output folder, then click the Save button. By naming the file with a unique name, the original ElectricCello file is retained.

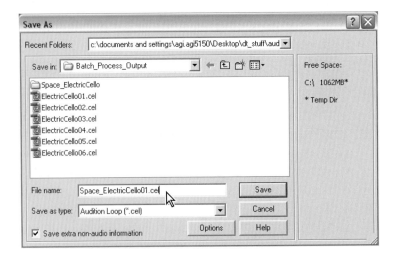

17 Double-click the ElectroCello02 file and choose File > Save As and navigate to the ElectricCello_Space folder if needed. Name the file you are saving ElectricCello02_Space.cel and click the Save button.

Using the Batch Processor

Running scripts on individual files is a quick way to apply multiple effects to a single waveform. When you need to apply a script to more than two or three files at a time, it is more efficient to use Audition's Batch Processing feature.

1   If necessary, switch to the Edit View by clicking on the Edit View tab. It is necessary to use the Edit View because Batch Processing is not available in the Multitrack View.

2   Choose File > Batch Processing and the Batch Processing window opens. Note at the bottom of the window there are 5 tabs; Files, Run Script, Resample, New Format, and Destination. These tabs represent the five steps you need to follow in order to successfully complete a Batch Process.

3   Click the Add Files button to open the Choose Source Files window. Navigate to the Batch_Process_Output folder located within the AA10 folder. This is the folder that contains the six ElectricCello samples you exported earlier in the lesson. We are only adding files 3-6 because you manually ran the script in the last exercise. To select the group of files, click on the file ElectricCello3.cel file, and then shift-click the ElectricCello6.cel file. Click the Add button to load these files into the Batch Processing window. Click the Hide Path option to see the short names of the files.

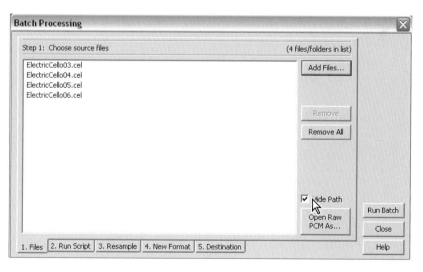

4   At the bottom of the Batch Processing window, click the second tab, Run Script. If necessary, select the Run a Script option. The first field points to a Script collection file. You created a script collection file named myCIBscripts.scp earlier in this lesson. If you do not see this script collection file click the browse button and locate the Scripts folder in your Audition 1.5 folder.

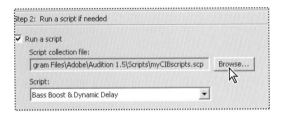

5   Along the bottom of the window, click the Resample tab. In the Resample tab, confirm the Conversion Settings checkbox is not selected. The conversion settings would allow you to convert files with different sample rates, bit depth and number of channels into one consistent setting, however you will not be converting in this exercise.

6   Click the New Format tab along the bottom of the window. Click on the Output Format drop-down menu to open it and choose Audition Loop (*.cel). Using this option you can convert all the files into a new format when using the Batch Processing command.

7 Click on the Destination tab along the bottom of the window. If necessary, select the Other Folder option and then click the Browse button. Navigate to the Batch_Process_Output folder in your AA10 folder. Click the plus sign and then click to select the ElectricCello_Space folder. Click OK to confirm the destination.

8 In the Output Filename Template type *_Space.cel. When creating a template, pay attention to the placement of the asterisk, as the asterisk will append the corresponding section of the filename. For example, ElectricCello03.cel will become ElectricCello03_Space.cel, and ElectricCello04.cel will become ElectricCello04_Space.cel.

9 Click the Run Batch button. The Bass Boost & Dynamic Delay script is run and applied to all of the selected files. The files are exported to the specified folder, in the file format you selected. Audition displays a window to confirm it is done.

10 To open the modified files and confirm the changes, choose File > Open and select the ElectricCello_Space folder. Click on ElectricCello03_Space.cel file, then shift-click on ElectricCello06_Space.cel. Click Open to import these 4 files into the Organizer window.

11 Double-click on ElectricCello06_Space.cel and press the spacebar. As you listen to the file you should note the dynamic delay effect and the bass lift that was applied using the batch process.

12 Choose File > Close All to close the session and its media.

Review questions

1   What are cue ranges, how do you create them, and how do they relate to Scripts?

2   How are scripts beneficial when using Adobe Audition?

3   Where is the Batch Processor located and when would you use it?

Review answers

1   Cue ranges are subsections of a larger waveform and allow you to identify and quickly move to portions of your sound files. Cue ranges are created by creating a selection in the Edit View and then defining the range in the Cue List. Cue ranges can be selected from the original waveform and saved as individual files through a Batch Process.

2   Use scripts to save a series of actions, such as copying data or applying an effect. You can then perform these actions with a single click, avoiding repetitive tasks. Scripts are stored text files that are similar to macros. Adobe Audition stores the actions you take and any parameters you modify, so you can repeat the sequence on a large number of files when running the script.

3   The Batch Processor is located in the File menu within the Edit View. The Batch Processor is similar to running a script, except the batch processing is performed on a series of files, rather than an individual file.

On your own

1　Open the Electric_Cello_Source file and use your selection tools to define different sections of the file. Create new cue ranges and export the ranges as separate files.

2　Using the exported files you created in the last step, or using the original ElectricCello.cel files, create your own script and add it to your myCIBscript collection. Examples of effects you may want to script are the Chorus effect or Amplify effect. Try experimenting with adding more then one effect in script; also pay careful attention to the order in which the effects are added. You will see different results based on the sequence in which the effects are used.

3　Run a script on the original Electric_cello.cel files using the File > Batch Processing command. In step 3 of the process select the Conversion Setting check box and then click on the Change Destination Format button. Experiment with saving the files as Mono files and converting the files to lower sample rates.

11 | Optimizing Audio Files For the Web

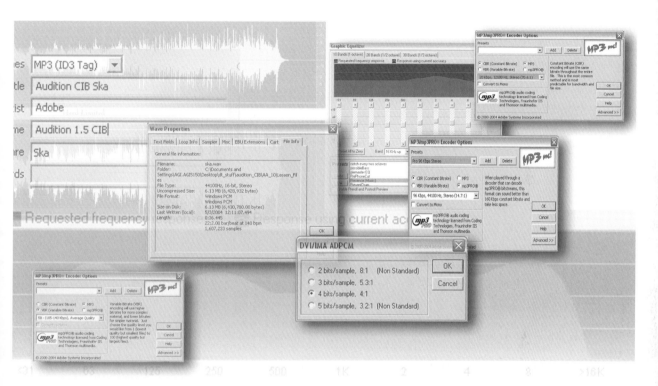

Distributing music files over the Internet requires special considerations. Audition allows you to effectively compress audio files based on the needs of your projects. Equalization, normalization, and hard limiting controls allow you to maximize the sound quality of your audio files that are delivered via the Internet.

In this lesson, you'll learn how to do the following:

• Use group normalize.

• Apply compression.

• Use Equalization.

• Batch Process using mp3 compression.

Getting started

1   Start Adobe Audition.

Note: If you have not already copied the resource files for this lesson onto your hard disk from the AA_11 folder from the Adobe Audition 1.5 Classroom in a Book CD, *do so now. See "Copying the Classroom in a Book files" on page 2.*

2   If necessary, select the Multitrack View tab to switch to this view.

3   Open the session 11_start.ses by choosing File > Open Session.

Reducing file size for the Internet

One of the unique challenges when it comes to working with audio files is that the same music track may be played in different environments. The qualities of sound that are audible when listening through a pair of headphones are different than when listening using a basic car radio. In general, audio engineers attempt to mix tracks that sound acceptable in a variety of situations. Creating audio files for distribution over the Internet provides another element of complexity: file size. A three-minute song saved in the WAV format may be 30 megabytes in size. Transferring files of this size is time-consuming and impractical. Fortunately, Audition provides methods to reduce file size while maintaining acceptable levels of fidelity. In this lesson you will examine some of the methods used to reduce file size, including changing the sample rate, reducing bit-depth, and applying compression. You will export a source file using a variety of methods to better understand how reductions in file size correlate to a reduction of quality.

1   In the Organizer window double-click on the ska.wav file to open the waveform into Edit View.

2 Choose View > Wave Properties to open the Wave Properties window. Using the Wave Properties command, you will add extra user-added text information to an audio file as well as view important file information. Keep the Wave Properties window open.

3 Click on the File Info tab. Important information about the file is located in this window. You can see that this is a 44100 Hz, 16 Bit, Stereo WAV file. In addition, the file format is Windows PCM, which is a specific type of a WAV file. Audition uses the PCM format as its default method for saving WAV files because it is considered a lossless format, where sound quality is not affected. The uncompressed file size is displayed as 6.13 megabytes. The value for the size on disk is exactly the same, because there was no compression applied to this file. Compressed files may show a smaller size on disk than when they are uncompressed.

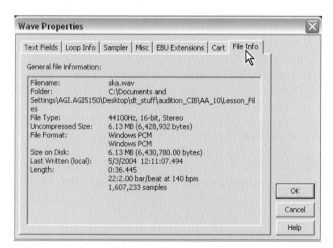

4 Click the OK button to close the Wave Properties window. Choose File > Save Copy As. In the Save Copy As window, choose DVI/IMA ADPCM (*.wav) from the Save as Type pull down menu. Enter **ska_DVI_ADPCM.wav** in the File name field. Keep the window open.

5   Click the Options button and the DVI/IMA ADPCM window opens, presenting four options: 2 bits/per sample through 5 bits per sample. Confirm that the 4 bits/sample option is selected. Click the OK button to close the DVI/IMA ADPCM window, but keep the Save Copy As window open.

About bit depth

The bit depth of a file determines the amplitude resolution. A bit is a computer term meaning a single number that can have a value of either zero or one. A single bit can represent two states, such as on and off. Two bits together can represent four different states: zero/zero, one/zero, zero/one, or one/one. Each additional bit doubles the number of states that can be represented, so a third bit can represent eight states, a fourth 16, and so on.

Amplitude resolution is just as important as frequency resolution. Higher bit depth means greater dynamic range, a lower noise floor, and higher fidelity. When a waveform is sampled, each sample is assigned the amplitude value closest to the original analog wave. With a resolution of two bits, each sample can have one of only four possible amplitude positions. With three-bit resolution, each sample has eight possible amplitude values. CD-quality sound is 16-bit, which means that each sample has 65,536 possible amplitude values. DVD-quality sound is 24-bit, which means that each sample has 16,777,216 possible amplitude values.

—From Adobe Audition Help

6   Navigate to the AA_11 folder and open the Compressed_Export subfolder. Click the Save button. If a warning message appears indicating that you are saving to a lower fidelity format, click OK to close the window.

This window appears the first time you save a file at a lower compression rate. You can check the Don't display this message in the future option to prevent this window from opening. However, leaving it unchecked acts as a safeguard, ensuring you do not save compressed files unless you intentionally choose to do so.

7   Double-click in an empty area of the Organizer window, opening the import window. If necessary, navigate to the AA_11 folder and then select the ska_DVI_ADPCM.wav file you exported earlier, and then click the Open button. In the Organizer window, double-click the ska_DVI_ADPCM.wav file to open it into the Edit View. In the Edit View, right-click on the waveform representing the file and choose Wave Properties from the context menu. In the Wave Properties window, the value for the Uncompressed Size remains at 6.13 Mb, however the value for the Size on Disk has been reduced to 1.53 Mb. This is a result of the 4:1 compression applied to the file at the time it was saved. The uncompressed file is four times larger than the compressed file.

8   Click the OK button to close the Wave Properties window. Press the spacebar on your keyboard to play the compressed ska file. After 5 seconds, press the spacebar again to stop playing the file. Double-click the original ska.wav in the Organizer window to open the waveform and press the spacebar to listen to the file for five seconds. Return to the compressed file by double-clicking on ska_DVI_ADPCM.wav, press Play to hear the file. You may not hear a significant difference in the two files, however the file size of the ska_DVI_ADPCM.wav file is approximately 75% smaller.

Compressing files in the mp3 format

The file you compressed in the previous exercise was only 54 seconds in length. Songs and audio clips are often much longer, and would create a much larger file, even when using the ADPCM .wav compression method. To allow for the additional compression that is necessary to effectively use longer sound files, the mp3 and, more recently, the mp3Pro technologies were developed. These file formats maximize sound quality while reducing file size. In this exercise you will apply different compression modes using Audition's mp3 encoding tools.

1   In the Organizer window, double-click the ska.wav file to load it into Edit View.

2 Choose File > Save Copy As. From the Save As Type drop-down menu choose mp3Pro from the list of available file formats. In the File Name field enter **20_Kbps. mp3**. Click the Options button and the mp3/mp3Pro Encoder Options window opens. If necessary, select the mp3 option and confirm that the Convert to Mono checkbox is not selected. Keep the mp3 Encoder Options window open.

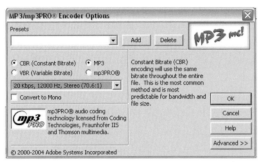

The mp3 Encoder Options window.

3 Choose 20 Kbps, 12000 Hz, Stereo (70.6:1) from the drop-down menu in the middle of the mp3 Encoder Options window (not the Presets menu at the top). The first value, 20 Kbps, refers to the Bitrate which is measured in Kilobits per second. Bitrate is the average number of bits that one second of audio data will consume. Higher bitrates produce larger file sizes and generally create better audio quality. The second value of 12,000 Hz refers to the sampling rate. The sampling rate of the original wav file is 44,100 Hz.

4 Click OK in the mp3 Encoder Options window. In the Save Copy As window, which is still open, navigate to the Compressed_Export folder located in the AA_11 folder on your hard drive. Click the Save button.

5 Double-click in an empty area of the Organizer window, and the import window opens. Select the ska_20Kbps.mp3 file you exported and then click the Open button. In the Organizer window, double-click the ska_20Kbps.mp3 file to open it in Edit View. Right-click on the waveform and choose Wave Properties. Note the value for the Uncompressed Size is now 1.67 mb.

The size is significantly smaller because the sample rate was reduced from 44,100 Hz to 12,000 Hz. Looking at the Size on Disk, note the size is 89.39 KB which is a result of setting the bitrate to 20 Kbps. This file is now 1/70th of the original file size. The size was first reduced by changing the sampling rate from 44,100 Hz to 12,000 Hz, and then further reduced by changing the bitrate to 20 Kbps.

What is sampling rate?

The sampling rate determines the frequency range of an audio file. The higher the sampling rate, the closer the shape of the digital waveform will be to that of the original analog waveform. Low sampling rates limit the range of frequencies that can be recorded, which can result in a recording that poorly represents the original sound.

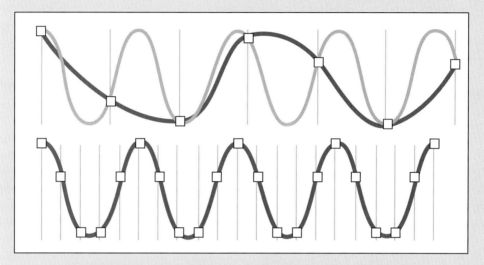

Two sample rates are displayed above. The top is an example of a low sample rate that distorts the original sound wave. The bottom shows a high sample rate that perfectly reproduces the original sound wave.

To reproduce a given frequency, the sampling rate must be at least twice that frequency. For example, if the audio contains audible frequencies as high as 8,000 Hz, you need a sample rate of 16,000 samples per second to represent this audio accurately in digital form. This calculation comes from the Nyquist Theorem, and the highest frequency that can be reproduced by a given sample rate is known as the Nyquist Frequency. CDs have a sample rate of 44,100 samples per second that allows sampling up to 22,050 Hz, which is higher than the limit of human hearing, 20,000 Hz.

6   Click OK to close the Wave Properties window and then press the spacebar to play the ska_20Kbps.mp3 file. The compression has adversely affected the audio quality of the file. The instruments have become muddy and indistinct, and the higher frequencies of the song, such as those in the drums, have deteriorated.

Using high-quality headphones when working with compression allows your ear to notice more of the artifacts and distortion created by compression. You should listen to completed files through both headphones and speakers before distributing the completed track.

7 Double-click on the ska.wav file in the Organizer window to open it into the Edit View. Choose File > Save Copy As. Enter the name **ska_50VBR.mp3**. Click the Options button to open the mp3 Encoder Options window. Select the VBR (Variable Bit Rate) radio button option and choose 50 (105-140 Kbps), Average Quality from the drop-down menu. Make certain that the mp3 option is selected. Keep the mp3 Encoder Options window open.

Variable Bit Rate

Variable Bit Rate or VBR is a technique which analyzes the audio file being encoded and uses higher bitrates for areas of higher complexity such as the crescendo of many instruments during a symphony. Conversely, areas of the same audio file which have less information, such as a trumpet solo, use lower bitrates. When you choose a level of compression, you are actually choosing a range of bitrates. Files encoded with VBR are less predictable in terms of file size than files encoded with Constant Bit Rate (CBR), this is because the file size is dependent on the type of music being encoded. In addition, not all mp3 players support files encoded with VBR. If you are planning on distributing mp3 files to the widest possible audience, you should stick with CBR encoded files, which may be larger in size but are more compatible.

8 In the Preset section of the mp3 Encoder window, click on the Add button to open the Add Preset window. In the Name Field enter **VBR (50 Quality) mp3 format**. By adding this custom preset, you are adding to those that are included with Adobe Audition. Click OK to close the Add Preset window and then click OK to close the mp3 Encoder window. Finally click the Save button to save the file into your AA_11 folder.

9 Double-click in an empty area of the organizer window to open the Import window. Choose the ska_50VBR.mp3 file you created earlier and then click the Open button. In the Organizer window, double-click the ska_50VBR.mp3 file to open it in Edit View. Using your keyboard, press Ctrl + P to open the Wave Properties window. While the uncompressed size remains at 6.13 mb, the actual file size on disk has been compressed to approximately 480 k. Click OK to close the Wave Properties window.

10 In the Organizer window, double-click on the ska.wav to open the file into the Edit View. Choose File > Save Copy As. Enter the name for this file as **ska_pro96Kbps.mp3**. Click the Options button to open the mp3 Encoder Options window. In the Presets field choose the Pro 96 Kbps Stereo option from the drop-down menu. This preset uses the mp3Pro technology. Click OK in the mp3 Encoder Options window and then click Save in the Save Copy As window to save the ska_pro96Kbps.mp3 file into your AA_11 folder.

> *mp3Pro Technology*
>
> *mp3Pro technology is a relatively new compression technique. Files encoded with mp3Pro use much lower bitrates than standard mp3 compression. The most common bitrates for standard mp3 files are 192Kbps, 160Kbps and 128Kbps. The latter is emerging as the de facto standard for files distributed on the Internet. mp3Pro on the other hand generally uses bitrates no higher than 96Kbps, although 80Kbps and 64Kbps are popular as well. The technology behind mp3Pro is called spectral band replication (SBR) which splits the audio file into low and high frequencies. The low frequencies are compressed at low bitrates, high frequencies are not compressed at all but are reconstructed by the playback device.*
>
> *mp3Pro files are backwards compatible with standard mp3 players, however there is a potential downside. mp3 Players which do not have mp3Pro capability will simply ignore the high frequency SBR data, which results in reduced sound quality. If you will be using mp3Pro technology you should check your software compatibility to make the most of this format.*

11 Double-click in any empty area of the Organizer window to open the Import window. In the Import window, select the ska_pro96Kbps.mp3 file and click Open. In the Organizer window, double-click the ska_pro96Kbps.mp3 file to open it in the Edit View. Press Ctrl + P to open the wave properties window. The uncompressed file is 6.14 mb and the file size is approximately 428 kb. This file and the file ska_50VBR.mp3 that you created previously have approximately the same file size, although they use two different forms of compression. Click OK to close the Wave Properties window.

Optimizing Sound Quality

In the previous exercise you used several techniques for compressing large audio files. This makes the files more manageable for distribution on the web. Regardless of the level of compression you use, a loss of audio data always occurs when compressing files. It is important to choose the compression technique that best suits the needs of your target audience. For example, an online news web site may sacrifice audio quality when compressing interviews under the assumption that the reduced file size outweighs the degradation to audio quality that occurs. Conversely, a band sending an mp3 file to a talent agent may decide to compress at a higher bitrate to achieve higher audio quality. In this exercise you use techniques that can improve the sound of audio files which will eventually be compressed. The three techniques you will be using are Equalization, normalization and hard limiting.

1　If you are not currently in the Edit View, click on the Edit View tab. Double-click in an empty area of the Organizer window to open the Import window. Navigate to the pachebel_wedding.wav file located in your AA_11 folder and click the Open button to place the file into your Organizer window. This is an uncompressed PCM wav file.

2　Double-click the pachebel_wedding.wav file to open it into Edit View. Choose Effects > Filters > Graphic Equalizer to open the Graphic Equalizer window. In the Graphic Equalizer window, confirm that the 10 bands (1 octave) tab is selected.

Graphic Eq is extremely useful when optimizing files for the web because the process of compression can introduce noise or unwanted artifacts in the higher frequencies.

3　In the Presets section, use the up or down arrows as necessary to scroll through the list of presets and choose Presence (music). Using this preset as a starting point, click the last slider, labeled >16k, and drag it to the bottom, reducing the highest frequencies.

4　Click the first slider, labeled <31, and drag it to the bottom as well. As you drag the slider to the bottom, the values for the gain are updated. Modifying the frequency levels also changes the overall volume of the file.

5 In the Graphic Equalizer window, set the following values for the remaining eq bands by using the up or down arrows for each band or by entering the Gain value:

• 63 , -8.9db

• 125, 1.0db

• 250, 6.4db

• 500, 0.2db

• 1k, 2.6db

• 2k, 8.4db

• 4k, 5.59db

• 8k, -10db

6 In the Master Gain text field enter **-4dB**. This reduces the overall volume of the waveform while maintaining the EQ relationships.

Note: For best results, experiment with these settings for different genres of music and for different songs. Settings that work well for one song may not work well for other songs.

7 Press the Preview button to play the file. Select the Bypass checkbox located directly above the Preview button at any point to temporarily remove the Graphic eq effect. Deselect the Bypass checkbox again to continue previewing the file with the effect applied.

8 Click the Add button in the presets section. Enter **Web Settings Classical** for the preset name, and then click OK.

9 Click OK in the Graphic Equalizer window and the EQ effects are applied. The waveform changes slightly due to the change in frequency value.

10 Choose File > Save As and rename this file **pachebel_wedding_eq.wav**. This saves the modified version without changing the original file. Click the Save button.

11 Choose Effects > Amplitude > Normalize and enter **85%** in the Normalize To field. Using Normalize you can raise the level of the entire waveform by an equal amount. A Normalization of 100% results in the maximum amplitude being applied to the WAV file. For files destined for the web, be careful using normalization values higher than 85%. Higher values may create clipping, which can sound very unpleasant to the human ear.

12 Click OK and the visual representation of the entire waveform displayed in the Edit View increases in height.

13 Choose Effects > Amplitude > Hard Limiting. In the Hard Limiting window, leave the default values unchanged. Click OK and note the entire waveform increases in amplitude.

Hard limiting increases the perceived volume of an audio file by compressing the distance between the loudest sections of the waveform and the quietest sections. Even though the sound is louder, there will not be any clipping because the loudest sections are "limited" to a specified level.

14 Press the Play button to preview the song. Although the song is loud, there is no distortion of the audio.

Compressing multiple files with the Batch Processor

Although individual files can be saved in the mp3 format as needed, you may need to convert a large number of files using the same settings. Adobe Audition's Batch Processor helps you accomplish this.

1 If necessary, switch to the Edit View. Choose File > Batch Processing and the Batch Processing window opens. You will be selecting a group of files to process.

2 In the Batch Processing window, click the Add Files button and navigate to the AA_11 folder on your had disk. Click on the first file DanceCryTrance.wav, and then shift-click on the last file ska.wav. All the WAV files in the folder should be selected. Click the Add button.

3 In the Batch Processing window, click the New Format tab located at the bottom of the window.

4 From the Output Format menu, choose mp3Pro, and then click the Format Properties button to open the mp3 Encoder Options window. From the Presets menu choose 128 Kbps Stereo (Internet) and click OK.

5 In the Batch Processing window, click on the Destination Tab located at the bottom of the window. Select the Same as file's source folder option, then click the Run Batch button. Audition converts the four WAV files into mp3 files using a bitrate of 128 Kbps and then places the files in the same folder from which the source files originated.

6 Click OK to close the Batch Processing progress window.

Review questions

1   How can you determine the compression used on any file?

2   What are sample rate and bit depth and how do they affect the size of a file?

3   What methods can you use to improve sound files which need to be heavily compressed, possibly for distribution via the Internet?

Review answers

1   Opening any file into the Edit View and choosing View > Wave Properties will open the Wave Properties window. Clicking on the File Info tab will access information about the file, including the Uncompressed Size and the Size on Disk.

2   Sample rate is the number of samples per second and it determines the frequency range of a file. The limit of human hearing on the high end of the frequency range is approximately 20,000 Hz. Low sampling rates reduce the range of frequencies in a file. CDs have a sample rate of 44,100 Hz. Lower sample rates reduce the size of a file but also reduce the quality of the file. Bit depth is defined as the number of bits used to represent audio amplitude. Higher bit depth means greater dynamic range and higher fidelity. Audition uses 32 bit depth by default. Lower bit depths give you smaller file sizes but lower quality files.

3   Equalization, normalization and hard limiting are three methods you can use to optimize files destined for the Internet. Equalization allows you to cut the higher frequencies in a file. Higher frequencies are particularly affected by heavy compression. Normalization is the process of increasing the amplitude of the highest peak in your file; which makes your file louder. Hard limiting increases perceived loudness, and heavily compressed files typically sound better.

On your own

1   Open the DanceCryTrance.wav file from the AA_11 folder and save a copy using the File > Save Copy As. Save the new copy as an mp3 and experiment with changing the bitrate and the sample rate through the mp3 Encoder Options, determine which combination sounds the best to you.

2   Choose File > Batch Processing and select the music files located in your AA_11 folder. Output the files as Windows Media Audio, be sure to click on the Format Properties button in the New Format tab.

12 | Importing CD Audio and Building a CD

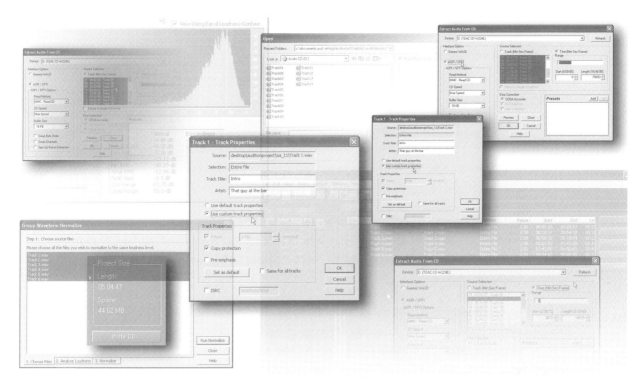

Audition's advanced audio extraction features provide options for importing and extracting audio files. You can also add text labels and track information for your custom CD projects.

In this lesson, you'll learn how to do the following:

• Use the CD Project View.

• Extract audio tracks from CDs.

• Set track properties.

• Normalize a group of tracks.

• Burn a Red Book compliant audio CD.

Getting started

Using the CD Project View you can engineer and create a professional quality audio CD from session files you've created, or from tracks you've extracted from your own CD library. You can also use Audition to extract pieces of audio tracks, or samples, which can be organized in the CD Project View.

Note: There are no lesson files for this lesson in the data portion of the CD to copy for this lesson. The Adobe Audition 1.5 Classroom in a Book *CD is a Mixed Media CD that includes both audio and data tracks. In this lesson you will be working with the audio components of the CD.*

Some CD-Rom drives may not be able to display the contents of a Mixed Media CD properly. To complete the following exercises in Adobe Audition, it may be necessary to substitute any standard audio CD for the Adobe Audition 1.5 Classroom in a Book *CD.*

Extracting Audio from a CD

Using the Extract Audio from CD command provides more refined control over what is extracted from an audio CD. Use this method to extract entire tracks or individual tracks. Once extracted, individual tracks can be combined into one continuous waveform.

The Extract Audio from CD command also provides for isolating specific ranges within an audio CD.

1   Start Adobe Audition. If necessary, insert the *Adobe Audition 1.5 Classroom in a Book* CD into the CD ROM drive of your computer. If a window opens asking what action to take with the CD, click the Cancel button.

2   Click the CD Project View tab, then choose File > Extract Audio from CD. A window opens for you to choose an audio file.

3   In the Extract Audio from CD window, choose the drive on your computer that contains the CD from the Device drop-down menu.

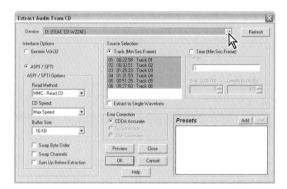

4   For Source Selection choose the Time option to extract part of Track01. Input a Start value of **0** and a Length value of **475**. Notice the time indicator above at 0:06:25 indicating a clip of 6.25 seconds in length will be extracted.

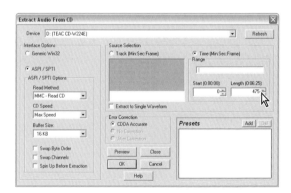

Note: *Selecting the Track option under Source Selection allows for the extraction of entire tracks from your audio CD.*

5 The actual start and length times appear in Min:Sec:Frame format above their respective boxes. The beginning frame appears in the Start box, and the total number of frames you wish to extract in the Length box. Each second of CD audio has 75 frames.

The Range bar provides a graphical representation of how much audio will be extracted and where the audio is located within the CD. Selecting a small amount of audio for extraction may not result in any change in the Range bar that is displayed. Notice that the range displayed is also relative to its location on the CD.

The Time option can be used for pulling hidden tracks from CDs, as well as for joining tracks that have been broken up by track indexes, such as performance track CDs and live albums.

6 In the Interface Option portion of the Extract Audio from CD window, confirm that the ASPI/SPTI option is selected. Leave the other fields in this section of the window unchanged.

Note: *The default Read Method, MMC—Read CD, is a SCSI-3 compliant format and works with most modern CD drives.*

Error correction when ripping a CD

If the CD-ROM drive you are using has built-in ripping error correction, CDDA Accurate is automatically selected for Error Correction. For these types of drives, no error correction is needed, so you won't be able to select any options from this part of the Extract Audio from CD dialog box.

If your drive isn't CDDA Accurate, you can select the No Correction and Jitter Correction options. No Correction results in no error correction as the CD is ripping. Jitter Correction compensates for data reading problems that older drives may encounter when reading a CD.

7 Listen to the selected portion of the track by clicking the Preview button.

8 Click OK to start extracting the audio file. Once Audition has completed ripping your audio selection, the file is listed in the files tab of Organizer window, as untitled*. You can then save the file from Edit View as a .cel file or any other audio file format.

9 Click on the file in the Organizer window to select it, then delete it from your session file by pressing the Delete key on your keyboard. A window opens, asking if you want to save the file, click No.

10 Choose File > Extract Audio from CD. In the Extract Audio from CD window that opens, choose the drive that contains the CD from the Device drop-down menu.

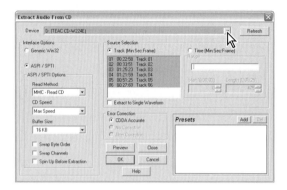

Confirm the Track (Min:Sec:Frame) radio button is selected and select only the following tracks to be ripped:

- Track01

- Track02

- Track03

- Track04

11 Click OK to extract the files into your CD project.

Once the files are extracted they are listed in the Files tab of the Organize window. The files have been converted into editable waveforms.

12 Select File > Save Session and save the session file into the AA_12 folder of your hard disk, naming the session **extracted_files.ses**.

Opening tracks from CDs

If your computer's CD-ROM drive supports audio digital extraction (also known as ripping), you can extract tracks from audio CDs. Extracting puts the audio into a waveform format which Adobe Audition can edit like any other waveform.

Adobe Audition provides two methods for ripping tracks from CDs: the Open command and the Extract Audio from CD command. The Open command is the fastest method and is preferred for ripping entire tracks. The Extract Audio from CD command provides more control, such as the ability to rip partial tracks and to specify the process used when extracting the file.

1 *Place an audio CD from your personal collection in the computer's CD-ROM drive.*

2 *Start Adobe Audition. Click the Edit View tab and then choose File > Open.*

3 *Choose CD Digital Audio (*.cda) as the file type, and navigate to the computer's CD-ROM drive.*

4 *Select the tracks to be ripped.*

5 *Click Open to extract the files into your CD project.*

Once the files are extracted they are listed in the Files tab of the Organize Window. The files have been converted into editable waveforms.

6 *Choose File > Save Session and save the session file onto your hard disk.*

Inserting and removing tracks

You will now organize the files in your CD Project by listing them in sequence in the CD Project View window. The order in which these files are listed is the sequence in which they will be played by an audio device. Audition allows you to add, remove or reorder files in the CD Project view.

There are a variety of ways to insert tracks into the CD Project View. Any file listed in the Files tab of the Organizer window can be added to a CD project. A file containing track cues can also be added to the CD project either by using the cue or the entire file.

1   Select the four .cda files now located in the Organizer window Track01 through Track04. Drag the items into the track list or click the Insert Into CD Project button.

💡 *You can drag any supported audio file type from your Windows desktop, including, My Computer, or Windows Explorer, directly into the track list in CD Project View. The file first opens in Adobe Audition, and then is inserted into the track list.*

To insert a session file from Multitrack View, open a session file, and choose Edit > Mix Down To CD Project. If the session includes track cues, each cue range is inserted into the track list as a separate track. If you want to divide a single, long audio file (such as a recording of a concert that includes several songs) into multiple tracks on a CD, insert the file into a session, and add track cues at the desired locations. Then, choose Edit > Mix Down To CD Project. The cue ranges are inserted automatically as separate tracks.

2   Using the Move Up or Move Down buttons on the right side of the CD Project View, you will reorganize your files to play in the following order of your new audio CD:

- Track04
- Track03
- Track02
- Track01

3   Delete Track04 from your CD Project by selecting it in the CD Project View window then clicking the Remove button.

Investigating the Project Size

The Project Size section of the CD Project View window displays the overall length of the tracks included in your CD Project, including the amount of available space.

Project Size info.

Setting track properties

Using Track properties, you can change the length of pauses between tracks, enable or disable copy protection and pre-emphasis features, and add an ISRC (International Standard Recording Code) number to your project. You can also specify a title and artist for each track for devices which support CD text display.

1 In CD Project View, select the Track01 , and click the Track Properties button. The Track Properties window opens.

2 In the Track Properties window enter a Track Title of **Song 1** and **Adobe Audition** for the Artist field of the window.

Note: For Adobe Audition to write text to a CD, the Write CD-Text option must be selected before burning the CD. This option appears in the Write CD window which you will see in the end of this chapter.

3 Click OK to close the Track Properties window.

Additional Track Properties

Additional properties can be set for each individual track by selecting each track, then selecting the Use Custom Track Properties button in the Track Properties window.

Pause—Adds a pause of the specified length before the track. By default, Adobe Audition assigns a 2-second pause to the beginning of each track.

Copy Protection—Sets the copy protection flag (as defined by the Red Book specification) for the track. In order for copy protection to occur, the CD player must support the copy protection flag.

Pre-Emphasis—Sets the pre-emphasis flag (as defined by the Red Book specification) for the track. Pre-emphasis is a basic noise reduction process that is implemented by a CD player. For pre-emphasis to occur, the CD player must support the pre-emphasis flag.

ISRC—Specifies an ISRC (International Standard Recording Code). This code is used only on CDs that are destined for commercial distribution. ISRC codes have 12 characters and use the following format:ISO Country: 2 digit code (for example, US for USA).

> *Registrant code: 3 digit alpha-numeric, unique reference.*
> *Year of reference: last 2 digits of the year (for example, 04 for 2004).*
> *Designation code: a 5 digit, unique number.*
> *Same For All Tracks: Applies all settings, except the ISRC code, to all tracks in the track list.*

—From Adobe Audition Help

Normalizing groups of files for mastering

When you assemble audio for a CD, you may want to fine-tune the individual tracks so that they are consistent with each other. Normalizing is a step in the overall process known as Mastering. Mastering may also involve cropping, adjusting dynamics, levels and EQ.

When you normalize a waveform, the loudest part of the waveform is modified to a specific amplitude, raising or lowering all other parts of the same waveform by the same amount. In this section you will use Group Waveform Normalize to normalize the volume of multiple open waveforms. Audition uses a three-screen batch process, providing control over statistical analysis, amount of normalization, and the files to which normalization is applied.

You will use Group Waveform Normalize to make sure that all tracks on the CD have a consistent volume.

1 While in CD Project View, choose Edit > Group Waveform Normalize.

2 Select each of the individual waveforms while holding the shift key from the Source Files portion of the window. All the waveforms become selected.

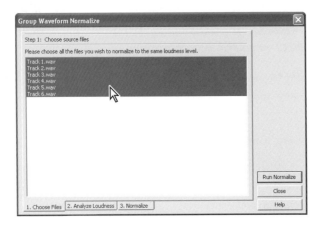

3 Click the Analyze Loudness tab at the bottom of the window, and then click the Scan for Statistical Information button to display amplitude statistics for each waveform.

💡 *Double-clicking a file in this list provides more detailed statistics, including an RMS histogram and a clipping profile. RMS, which stands for Root Mean Square, is an average of continuous power, measured in watts, which a wave source produces.*

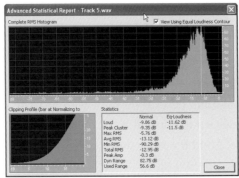

Advanced Statistical Report window accessed by double-clicking on a file.

4 Click the Normalize tab. Confirm that the Normalize to Average Level of Source Files option is selected and that the Use Limiting option is also selected.

Note: The option to Use Equal Loudness Contour reduces the apparent volume of frequencies that might otherwise be perceived as being louder than others.. Because the human ear is much more sensitive to frequencies between 2 kHz and 4 kHz, two different pieces of audio with the same RMS amplitude but with different frequencies will appear to have different volumes. This option ensures that audio has the same perceived loudness, regardless of the frequencies that are included in the recording.

5 Click the Run Normalize button. The original files are normalized, resulting in a more uniform and consistent group of waveforms ready for CD burning.

Writing a CD

Before writing a CD, you will verify that your CD burning device is set up correctly, set CD options and then write the CD. If you do not have a CD writer on your computer you can move ahead to the Review questions.

Audio on CDs must be 44.1 kHz, 16 bit, stereo. If you insert a track with a different sample type, Adobe Audition automatically converts the audio for you.

1 Insert a blank, writable CD into the CD drive of your computer.

2 In CD Project View, click the Write CD button or choose File > Write CD. The Write CD window opens.

3 Select the device you want to use to write the CD from the drop-down menu of available drives.

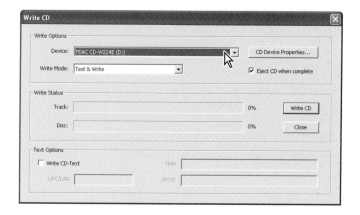

4   In the Write CD window, you have the option to select a setting from the Write Mode drop-down menu:

• Write CD writes the CD without testing for buffer underruns.

• Test only tests if the CD can be written without the occurrence of buffer underruns. No audio is written to the CD.

• Test and Write CD tests for buffer underruns and then proceeds with the actual write process if the test is successful.

5   Select Eject CD When Complete to eject the CD tray upon completion of the write process. Select the Write CD-Text to write the track title and artist for each track to the CD.

• If you have a UPC/EAN number, you can enter it here. The UPC/EAN is a 13-digit code that is used to uniquely identify merchandise and communicate product information between a vendor and retailer.

6   From the Write Mode drop-down menu, select the Write option, then check the Eject CD when complete checkbox option.

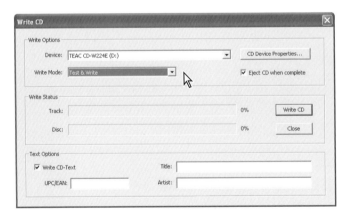

7   Click the Write CD button to write your tracks to CD. The Track and Disk bars show you the progress of the write process.

8   Once completed, test your CD in an audio CD player, or re-insert it into the CD drive of your computer and play the files using Windows Media Player.

Review questions

1   What file format is used for audio CD files?

2   What step ensures consistent amplitude across all audio tracks?

3   How can you ensure a consistent pause between tracks?

Review answers

1   CD audio (.cda) is the standard file format for audio CDs.

2   Audition's Group Waveform Normalize function allows several files to be processed so that relative amplitude is set to an average amount.

3   Using Custom Track Properties in the Track Properties window in CD Project View you can specify an exact time increment in between each track.

On your own

1   Locate an audio file of a long continuous recording. This could be a recording of a live concert, a speech, or combination of continuous songs.

2   Click on the Edit View tab and choose File > Open.

3   Locate the file and import into Adobe Audition.

4   Click on the Hide/Show Cue List button opening the Cue List window.

5   Play the file by pressing the spacebar, making note of the points at which you would like to insert track cues. Track cues break up a long waveform into smaller waveforms which can be independently used in a CD project file.

6   Locate the position of the first break in the waveform in which you'd like to place a track cue. Click and drag from the beginning of the waveform to isolate the first portion of the file.

7   Click the Add button in the Cue List window then select the Edit Cue Info button, expanding the window to include Cue Info.

8   Change the cue Type from Basic to Track from the drop-down menu, then label the cue accordingly.

9   Using the same process, insert cues throughout the rest of the waveform, naming each cue accordingly to its content.

10   Once you are finished inserting cues into your waveform, select the CD Project View tab.

11   Click on the plus sign (⊞) next to the original file listed in the Files tab of the Organize window, revealing all the labeled cues you've just created.

12   Right-click on each cue and select Insert into CD Project, or click and drag each cue into the CD Project view. Reorganize the cues by selecting the Move Up or Move Down buttons to sequence the cues in the order you wish them to be listed in your audio CD.

13   Click the Write CD button and then click OK.

13 | Integrating Adobe Audition and Adobe Premiere Pro

You can import high-quality audio files from Adobe Audition for use in Adobe Premiere Pro and easily modify audio files used in Adobe Premiere Pro by opening original multitrack sessions in Adobe Audition. You can also use noise reduction effects to clean up video soundtracks using Adobe Audition.

In this lesson, you'll learn how to do the following:

• Insert video files into Audition.

• Create a soundtrack to a video clip.

• Use the Edit Original command in Multitrack View.

• Use the Edit Original command in Edit View.

Getting started

Adobe Audition and Adobe Premiere Pro provide complementary tools for editing audio and video. In this lesson, you will use Audition's Multitrack View to create a soundtrack to a video clip. Additionally, you will use tools in Audition's Edit View to clean up, and work with, source audio files from Adobe Premiere Pro. Although Premiere Pro offers some mixing and effect capabilities, Audition's specialized audio tools allow you to extend your audio editing beyond the capabilities of Adobe Premiere.

Note: The first two sections of this lesson use Adobe Audition while the remaining sections require Adobe Premiere Pro. If you do not have Adobe Premiere Pro, you can download the trial version of Premiere Pro which is available online at http://www.adobe.com/products/ tryadobe/main.jsp

1 Start Adobe Audition. Click the Multitrack View tab if not already selected.

Note: If you have not already copied the resource files for this lesson onto your hard disk from the AA_13 folder from the Adobe Audition 1.5 Classroom in a Book CD, do so now. See "Copying the Classroom in a Book files" on page 2.

2 To review the finished session file from this lesson, choose File > Open Session. Navigate to the AA_CIB folder you copied to your hard disk, and open the file "AA13_ end.ses" in the AA_13 folder. Click the Play to End button (⊙) in the Transport Controls toolbar or press the spacebar on your keyboard. The completed file is played for you.

3 Close the 13_end.ses file by choosing File > Close Session and Its Media.

4 Choose File > New Session. In the New Session window, choose 48000 for the sample rate and then click the OK button. Choose File > Save Session As and name this session **AA13_start.ses**.

In this lesson you will be working with Premiere Pro. Premiere Pro uses the DV Playback mode and 48,000 Hz is the standard audio sample rate used in digital video projects. Using this sample rate allows for maximum compatibility with Premiere Pro.

Inserting Video into Audition

Audition can import a variety of video file formats, including AVI, native DV, MPEG and WMV files. You can also view the video component of movie files while in the Multitrack View. Using the Edit View, you can import only the audio portion of a movie file. Only one video file is displayed in the multitrack at a time.

1　Choose Insert > Video. Navigate to the AA_13 chapter files folder on your hard drive and click to select the file supercar.avi, click the Open button.

2　Audition inserts the video track into track one. As the file is imported, the Video window opens and the first frame of the movie clip is displayed.

The video file supercar.avi is a full-screen AVI file, with a resolution of 720 pixels wide by 480 pixels high. Audition displays video files at 100% of their original size the first time they are opened. Depending on the size of your monitor, the video window may cover most of your multitrack.

Note: If Audition did not automatically open a video window, choose Window > Video from the main menu. Based on the previous workspace you were using, Audition may insert the video window into another area of the interface.

3   Right-click in the center of the video window to open a context menu. The value of 100% displays a checkmark if you have not changed your default viewing percentage. From the context menu, choose 50% to reduce the dimensions of the video file by one-half.

4   Place your cursor in the lower right hand corner of the Video window until your cursor changes to a diagonal double arrow, and drag toward the center of the window to reduce the size. Like most windows in Audition, the Video window is fully resizable and can be docked.

5   To dock the Video window, click the title bar at the top of the window. Drag the window to the left. Place your cursor directly over the Effects tab in the Organizer window, then release your mouse. The Video window is added to the docking area.

Note: To remove the window from the docking area, place your cursor over the double bar at the top of the window and drag it out. The Video Window can also be docked in other areas of the Audition workspace.

6   To expand the viewing area of the docked Video window, place your cursor over the bottom of the docked window until it changes to a double arrow, then click and drag downwards to expand the window vertically.

7   Press the spacebar and the movie clip plays in the Video window. The video clip is approximately 15 seconds long and includes no audio track. When the video finishes, press the spacebar to stop the playback cursor.

Note: Although this AVI video clip has no audio track, Audition will import both the video and audio portion of any compatible video file.

8   Press the Home key to return the current-time indicator to the beginning of the timeline. Right-click on the timeline and from the context menu choose Display Time Format > SMPTE 29.97 fps. This changes Audition's time display to SMPTE timecode, a timing reference used to synchronize a camera with another device. SMPTE timecode is divided into hours, minutes, seconds, and frames, a standard method for measuring time for film and video.

9   Click on the Zoom to Selection tool (![icon]) to increase the magnification of the timeline. The time display changes as well. Audition displays image thumbnails of the video content. Click the Zoom to Selection tool again and the number of thumbnails increases as you increase the magnification.

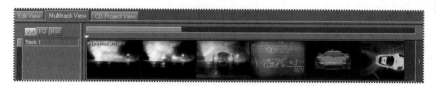

10 Click the Zoom Out Full Both Axis button (![icon]) to display the complete video file from start to finish. Press the spacebar to play the movie clip. As the file plays, the Video window display does not correspond to the exact position of the playback cursor. These thumbnails serve as a general guideline for positioning, and are not accurate to the specific frame of video being played.

11   Choose File > Import and navigate to the AA13 folder on your hard disk. Select the trance05.cel file and the SnareRoll02.cel file by Ctrl-clicking them, and click Open to import the files into the Organizer window. Choose the Multitrack View button () and in the Organizer window, click to select the trance05.cel clip and drag it into track 2.

12   If necessary, click and drag the clip to align it with the beginning of the track. Choose Edit > Snapping and if the option for Snap to Clips is not checked, select it now. Click the handle at the bottom right hand corner of the trance05 clip and drag to extend the loop to the right and align the end with the video clip in track 1.

13   Click and drag the current-time indicator to the 4 second 12 frame mark which is the point in the video where the animated equations begin to fade in.

14   From the Organizer window, click and drag the loop SnareRoll02.cel into track 3 and align the beginning of the clip with the current-time indicator.

15   In the Organizer window, double-click the SnareRoll02.cel file to display it in the Edit View. Press the Home key on your keyboard to move the playback cursor to the start of the clip. Press the Play button to play the file.

16 Choose Effects > Reverse in the main menu. Press the spacebar to hear the reversed sound effect. Playing a sound effect backwards is a simple and fast way to give it a distinctive sound.

17 Choose File > Save As and name this new file **BackwardsSnare.cel**. Navigate to the AA13 folder on your hard disk, then click the Save button. After the file has been saved, click on the Multitrack View tab. Renaming the snare drum file after adding the reverse effect is necessary in order to leave the original file untouched, the reverse snare drum is automatically updated in track 2.

18 Press the Home key on your keyboard to return the playback cursor to the start of the timeline, and then press the spacebar to play the session file. Synchronizing the reverse snare drum clip with the animated equation sequence creates a pleasing effect, however the snare drum clip is currently shorter than the middle section of the video. You will use Audition's Clip Time Stretching feature to correct that.

19 Click the Clip Time Stretching button (🔳) in the toolbar. This allows clips to be stretched. If necessary, choose View > Toolbars and confirm Multitrack View is selected to display the Clip Time Stretching button.

20 Click and drag the current-time indicator to the right. Observe the video window while moving the current-time indicator. Move the current-time indicator to the 7 second 15 frame point, which is the location where the animated equation fades out.

21 Click the handle on the bottom right hand corner of the BackwardsSnareRoll02 clip and drag to the right to stretch the clip to the current-time indicator.

Clip Time Stretching expands the length of the clip which has the effect of slowing down the sound of the clip without changing the pitch. The time stretch icon appears in the bottom left of the clip, indicating that the clip has been stretched.

22 Click on the Clip Time Stretching button (![icon]) to disable this feature.

23 Click and drag the Current-Time Indicator back to the 3 second mark in the timeline. Press the spacebar to play the file and listen to the effect of the time stretch. The backwards snare drum is now synchronized with the animated equation video sequence.

Inserting the Audio track only into Audition

In the previous exercise you imported an .AVI file into Audition. Audition is also capable of importing only the audio component of a video file.

You can use this feature to extract the audio portion of a recorded musical performance, or import the dialog from a video or film recording that needs to be improved. Because importing digital video and audio require more system resources than importing the audio alone, it is often more efficient to work exclusively with the audio. In this exercise you will import the audio track from a racing car video clip, and then use it as a sound effect in your session file. You will also use Audition's effects tools to alter the shape of the sound.

1 Click on track 4 to select it, press the Home key to place the current-time indicator at the beginning of the session and then choose Insert > Audio from Video.

2 In the Insert Audio from Video window, navigate to the AA13 folder and click to select the file racecar.avi, then click the Open button. The Extract Audio progress window appears as Audition extracts the audio portion of the AVI file and imports the file as racecar in the Multitrack View.

3   Click the solo button (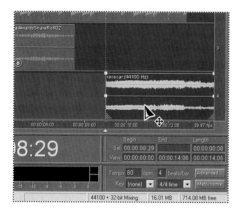) in track 4 and press the spacebar on your keyboard to hear the sound of the racing car that was extracted from the video clip. Later you will match the sound effect of the racing car to the final section of the movie clip.

4   Click and drag the current-time indicator to the 9 second mark. You should still have the Video window from the last exercise open. If not, choose Window > Video to reopen it. At the 9 second mark, the image of the car racing through the tunnel starts to appear.

5   Click to select the Multitrack View button (▦) then click and drag the beginning of the racecar sound clip so it is positioned at the Current-Time Indicator. Press the Play to End button (⊙) to hear the sound clip and watch the video

The position of the sound clip is synchronized with the video, but the original audio has a stereo pan from right to left and the video clip has the car exiting to the right side of the screen. This makes this audio and video combination distracting and unrealistic. You will now fix the pan properties to synchronize the movement of the car to the sound of the car.

6   Double-click the racecar clip in track 4 to open it into the Edit View. Choose Edit > Convert Sample Type. Click to select the Mono option and then click OK. The left and right channels of the stereo file are converted to a single mono channel.

7   Choose File > Save As and navigate to the AA_13 folder on your hard disk. Name the file **racecar.cel** and click OK.

8   Click on the Multitrack View tab to return to the Multitrack View. Now that the racecar has been converted to a mono file, you will be manipulating the pan properties to correspond with the video of the car exiting to the right side of the screen.

9   Click on the racecar.cel file to select it. Choose View and make sure Show Pan Envelopes is checked, if not, select it now. The Pan Envelope line appears down the center of the clip, indicating that the sound is located stereo center.

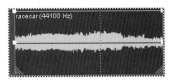

Clip with Pan and Volume
envelopes selected.

10   Click and drag the Current-Time Indicator to the 12 second mark in the timeline. At this point in the video the car starts to race off-screen. You will match the racecar sound effect to the video.

11   Click the Pan Envelope line at the 12 second mark to add an anchor point.

12   Click the anchor point at the end of the clip and drag it to the bottom of the clip. This positions the sound of the car to stereo right. Click the Pan Envelope line halfway between the two anchor points, adding a third anchor point. Click and drag the new anchor point down and to the left. As you drag, the pan values appear in a small window, we used the value of 65. This creates a pan effect that accelerates the transition to stereo right. To hear the effect of the pan, click and drag the Current-Time Indicator to the beginning of the racecar.cel clip and press the spacebar. The playback cursor stops at the end of the session.

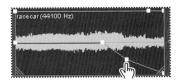

13   Track 4 should still be soloed, you want to be able to hear the music track in addition to the racecar effect, so click on the Solo button in track 4 and press the spacebar to play.

14 You will now fade in and out the sound of the racecar to make it even more realistic. If necessary, select the Volume Envelopes button () to enable them. The volume envelope line appears at the top of the racecar.cel clip. You should also click on the Pan Envelopes button to hide the line from your clip. The racecar clip should still be selected from the previous step, if it is not, simply click on it. Place your cursor over the anchor point on the top left corner of the clip. Click and drag this anchor point all the way to the bottom. This will create a gradual fade in from the beginning of the clip to the end.

15 Place your cursor on the volume envelope line and using the ruler as a guide click on the volume envelope at the 10 second mark to add an anchor point. Then click and drag this anchor point to the top of the clip. This creates a fade in.

16 To create a fade out, click on the volume envelope line at the 13 second mark to add an anchor point. Then click and drag on the last anchor point at the end of the clip all the way to the bottom.

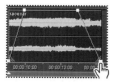

17 Press the Home key on your keyboard to place the current-time indicator at the start of the timeline. Click the Solo button on track 4 to enable the first three tracks. Press the spacebar to play the session from beginning to end.

18 Choose File > Save As... Name the file **AA13_mixdown.ses** and click OK.

Linking a Premiere audio clip to an Audition multitrack session

In this exercise you will switch between Adobe Audition and Adobe Premiere Pro. You will need to have Premiere Pro installed on your computer to perform the remaining portions of this lesson. You will use the Edit Original command, which links Audition session files to the corresponding WAV files used by Premiere Pro.

1   If you do not have the AA13_mixdown.ses file open from the last exercise, choose File > Open Session and open it now. Choose Options > Settings and the Settings window opens.

2   In the Settings window, click the Data tab and make sure the Embed Project Link data for Edit Original functionality check box is checked. If it is not checked, do so now. Click the OK button to close the Settings window. This ensures that Premiere Pro links your mixdown files to Audition. Choose File > Save Session to ensure that the Embed Project Link is saved.

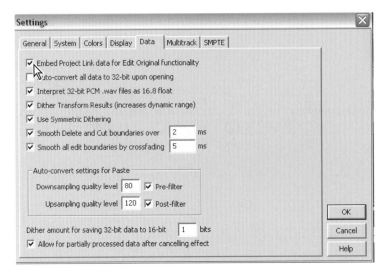

3   Choose File > Export > Audio. The Export Audio window opens.

4   Enter the name **audition_musictrack.wav** for this file. By default, Audition saves exported music tracks as Windows PCM wav files. If necessary, pull down the Save as Type menu and choose Windows PCM from the list. Keep the Export Audio window open. If necessary, click Yes to overwrite the existing file.

5   Confirm that the checkbox for Save extra non-audio information is selected. This checkbox must be checked in order to use the Edit Original command in Premiere. When selected, Audition saves the path to the session. Saving path information allows Premiere Pro and After Effects to link to original session and mixdown files.

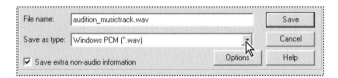

6   If necessary, navigate to your AA13 folder on your hard drive and click the Save button. Audition mixes down the tracks as a wav file and saves it to your hard disk.

7   Launch Adobe Premiere Pro. Click the Open Project folder option in the window that displays when you start the program. Navigate to your AA13 student folder and choose the Premiere project file Saleen_Edit_Original.prproj and then click Open. The Premiere Pro workspace opens, and the file supercar.avi is displayed in video track 1.

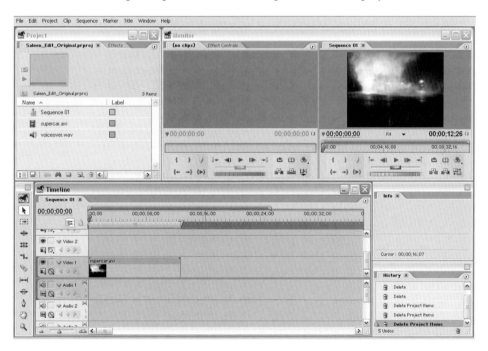

8   Double-click in an empty area of the Project window, to open the Import window. In the import window, navigate to the AA13 folder and select the **audition_musictrack. wav** file you just exported from Audition. Click the Open button to import the file into the Project window.

9   Click and drag the audition_musictrack clip from the Project window into the Audio 1 track. Click and drag the clip to the left, so the start of the audio clip is aligned with the start of the supercar video clip.

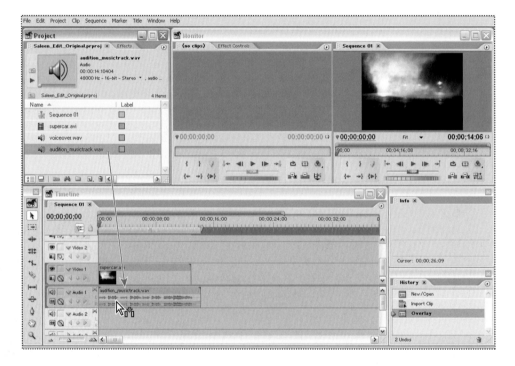

10   Click the Timeline to make it the active window. Press the Home key on your keyboard to move the current-time indicator to the start of the timeline. Press the spacebar to play the sequence. The soundtrack you created in Audition is synchronized with the racecar.avi file.

11   Right-click the audition_musictrack clip in the Audio track 1 to open the context menu. Choose Edit > Original. The Edit Original Options window opens. Confirm that the Launch Audition Multitrack Session option is selected and then click OK. The session AA13_mixdown.ses opens in Adobe Audition.

Note: *If the Edit Original Options window does not open, you may not have enabled the Edit Original feature. To enable the Edit Original feature, return to step 2 of this exercise and confirm you have selected the option which embeds the Project Link functionality. Additionally, an import option in step 5 is also necessary: wav files must have the Save extra non-audio information option selected in order to link from Premiere or After Effects.*

12 Choose File > Import and navigate to the AA_13 folder. Select the audio file RhodesOrgan.cel. Click the Open button to import the file into the Organizer window.

13 Click on the Zoom Out Vertically button (⌖) to view additional open tracks. Click on Track 5 to select it.

14 Click to select the RhodesOrgan clip in the Organizer window and then click and drag it into track 5.

15 Choose the Multitrack View button (⌗), drag the entire clip to the left so the beginning of the clip snaps to the beginning of the session, then click the handle on the bottom-right of the RhodesOrgan clip. Drag the handle to the right, extending the loop until the end of the clip matches the end of the drum loop in track 2.

16 Choose File > Save Session.

17 Choose File > Export > Audio. The Export Audio window appears. If necessary, navigate to the AA13 directory. You will overwrite the audition_musictrack.wav file that you saved in Step 6. In the File name field enter **audition_musictrack.wav**.

18 Click the Save button. The File Save window opens, informing you that you are overwriting an existing file. Click Yes to confirm that you want to replace the existing file. You are overwriting the original WAV file because you have added a new organ track that changed the session file.

19 Choose File > Exit to quit Adobe Audition.

20 Switch to Premiere Pro and click the Timeline window to make it the active window. If necessary, press the Home key to place the current-time indicator at the beginning of the session.Press the spacebar to play the timeline. The waveform has been automatically updated, and you now hear the RhodesOrgan track you added.

21 Choose File > Save to save the existing Premiere Project.

Opening a Premiere audio clip into Audition's Edit View

In the last exercise, you used the Edit Original command on a wav file in Premiere to launch an original multitrack session in Audition. You can also use the Edit Original feature to open a wav file directly into Audition's Edit View. Working with a file in Edit View allows you to make use of many Audition features, including noise reduction, studio reverb, parametric equalization and more. In this exercise you will open a voiceover file which was originally recorded in Audition, and remove an imperfection.

1 If you do not have the project from the last exercise still open in Premiere Pro, choose File > Open. Navigate to the AA_13 chapter files folder and choose the Saleen_Edit_Original.prproj.

2   In the Project window, double-click the file voiceover.wav. The voiceover.wav file opens in Premiere's Source Monitor as a waveform. Press the Play button in the Source window to listen to the voiceover file, which is 15 seconds in length. At the 5 second mark there is a small click in the file, perhaps from the narrator's chair or from another source in the studio. While Premiere may allow for editing this file, Audition's tool set makes the process much easier.

3   In the Project window, right-click the audio file voiceover.wav. From the context menu choose Edit Original. Adobe Audition opens and the wav file is automatically placed into Edit View and begins playing. There is no Audition session associated with this file, therefore it only opens in Edit View.

Note: Only files which are saved in Audition with the Embed Project link option are associated with the Audition application. Wav files from other sources may open in other programs based on your operating system preferences which link certain file types to specific programs. You can make Windows associate all wav files with Audition by right-clicking on a wav file and choose Open With > Choose Program. Select Adobe Audition and select the checkbox "Always use this selected program to open this kind of file."

4   Place your cursor at the 5 second mark in the timeline. Click and drag across the waveform to make a selection of approximately 15 frames. Use the Selection/View controls in the bottom right corner to help measure the selection. Press the spacebar on your keyboard to play the selection. You should be able to hear the click and the beginning of the narrator's next phrase following the click.

5   Click the Zoom to Selection button (🔍) and the selection is magnified in the display window. The click in the audio is visible as a peak in the waveform. Press the spacebar and the selection plays. You can visually match the sound of the click with its location in the waveform.

6   Choose View > Spectral View to see the audio in spectral view. The Spectral View displays the waveform based upon its frequency components: the x-axis (horizontal axis) represents time and the y-axis (vertical axis) measures frequency.

7   Choose the Marquee Selection tool (▦).

8   Press the spacebar to play the selection. Note how the click is represented by the red-colored frequency band at the 5 second 10 frame mark. Place your cursor at the top left of the frequency band and drag down to the right to draw a selection around the frequency band that represents the click sound.

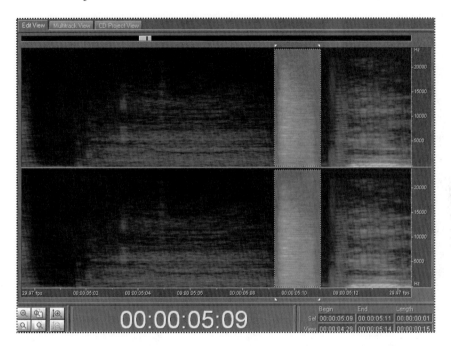

9   Press the spacebar on your keyboard to hear your selection. You should clearly hear the click as the selection plays.

10 Press the Delete key on your keyboard and the audio information in this frequency range is deleted. Press the spacebar and the click has been removed.

The overall length of the original waveform has not changed.

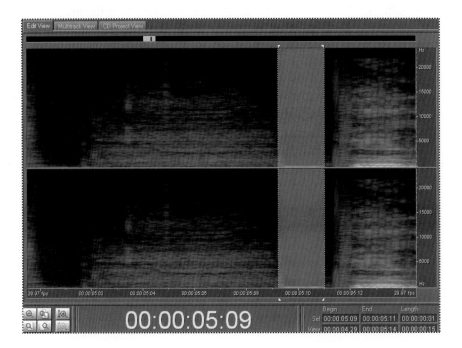

11 Choose View > Waveform View to return to the waveform view. Note the waveform reflects the removal of the click. Click the Zoom Out Full Both Axis button ( ) to view the entire waveform, click once at the 4 second mark to place your current-time indicator there and then press the spacebar on your keyboard to play the audio clip. The click from the original file has been removed.

12 Choose File > Save As. Enter the name **voiceover_repaired.wav** for this file and then click the OK button. Work performed in the Edit View is destructive. By renaming files that you have modified, you ensure that a backup remains available. If necessary click Yes to overwrite.

13 Choose File > Exit to quit Adobe Audition.

14 Switch to Premiere Pro. In the Project Window, click to select the voiceover.wav file. Click the trash can icon (🗑) to remove the file from the project window. This removes the original file with the click from the project window.

15 Double-click in the empty area of the Project window below the file list. The import window opens. Navigate to the AA13 folder and click to select the voiceover_repaired.wav file. Click the Open button to import the file into the project window. In the project window, double-click the file to load it into the Source Monitor view.

16 Press the spacebar to play the file. This file is the edited file and the click has been removed.

17 Click and drag the voiceover_repaired.wav file from the Source Monitor View directly into Audio Track 2. Make certain that the clip is aligned at the beginning of the track. Press the Home key to return to the beginning of the timeline and then press the spacebar to play the completed movie.

18 Save the Premiere project and exit Premiere Pro.

Review questions

1   What are the two methods of incorporating video into Audition?

2   What are the two necessary steps to ensure that exported wav files used in Premiere Pro or After Effects are linked to Audition session files?

3   How can you access Audition files while in Premiere Pro or After Effects?

Review answers

1   The first method of incorporating video into Audition is by inserting a video track into the Multitrack View. The following video formats are supported: AVI, native DV, MPEG and WMV files. You can preview video in the Multitrack View, improve audio quality and create original soundtracks with Audition's real-time looping and mixing capabilities. The second method is to import only the audio data from a video file, this is useful when the Video data is not necessarily needed.

2   The first step in Audition is choosing Options > Settings and then clicking on the Data tab. Then choose Embed Project Link Data For Edit Original Functionality. The second step is when the session file is exported as a wav file. You must select Save Extra Non-Audio Information in the Export Audio dialog box in order for the program to use the Edit Original command.

3   Both Premiere Pro and After Effects will open WAV files created in Audition through the Edit Original command. The user then has the choice to open the original session file in the Multitrack View of Audition, or alternatively, to open the exported audio file into the Edit View as a single waveform.

On your own

1   In the **AA13_mixdown.ses** file from the last exercise, practice using the volume envelopes you learned how to use in chapter 4, Working in the Multitrack View to create a fadeout on the RhodesOrgan clip you added to track 5. Additionally, you should explore how Audition can create an automatic fade in and fade out, create a selection in the RhodesOrgan clip and right-click on the clip to choose Crossfade. Explore the differences between applying the Linear, Sinusoidal and Logarithmic crossfades.

2   Create a new session at 48,000 Hz sample rate and using the racecar.avi clip, create a new soundtrack using the methods in the first exercise. Use at least three tracks with the clips provided for you on the Adobe Audition Loopology CD. The Loopology CD provides thousands of musical samples from all genres of music. When you are done creating the new soundtrack, choose Export > Audio to export the session as a WAV file. If you do not have Premiere, you have the option of choosing Export > Video in order to view your results.

3   Be sure you understand the process of linking mixdown wav files in Premiere Pro to Audition session files by exporting the new soundtrack you created, and importing it into the Saleen_Edit_Original.prproj used in the last exercise. Right-clicking on the wav file and choosing Edit > Original will automatically open Audition in either the Multitrack View or the Edit View, based on the user's choice.

Index

Production Notes

The Adobe Audition 1.5 Classroom in a Book was created electronically using Adobe InDesign CS. Art was produced using Adobe InDesign, Adobe Illustrator, and Adobe Photoshop. Proofing was completed using Adobe Acrobat 6 Professional using Adobe PDF files.

References to company names and telephone numbers in the lessons are for demonstration purposes only and are not intended to refer to or imply endorsement of any actual organization or person.

Typefaces used

Adobe Caslon Pro, Adobe Garamond Pro, Minion Pro, Myriad Pro and Trajan Pro are used throughout the lessons.

Production team credits

The following individuals contributed to the development of the *Adobe Audition 1.5 Classroom in a Book*:

Project coordinator, editor: Christopher G. Smith

Project writing and design: Jeremy Osborn and Luis Mendes

Production: AGI Training: Jennifer M. Smith, Patti Scully-Lane

Proofreading: Jay Donahue, Cathy Auclair

Testing: Greg Heald, Kelly Babik, Sean McKnight, Larry Happy

Thanks to Ken Gordon and Tad Lemire—Chapter 6; Tad Lemire and Amy Ryan of WCTK 98.1—Chapter 7; and Sam Davol—Chapter 10; Jason Levine—Lesson 12 CD audio tracks.

Training and inspiration from Adobe Press

Classroom in a Book
The easiest, most comprehensive way to master Adobe software! *Classroom in a Book* is the bestselling series of practical software training workbooks. Developed with the support of product experts at Adobe Systems, these books offer complete, self-paced lessons designed to fit your busy schedule.

Each book includes a CD-ROM with customized files to guide you through the lessons and special projects.

Real World Series
Get industrial-strength production techniques from these comprehensive, "under-the-hood" reference books. Written by nationally recognized leaders in digital graphics, Web, and new media, these books offer timesaving tips, professional techniques, and detailed insight into how the software works. Covering basic through advanced skill levels, these books are ideal for print and Web graphics pros.

Idea Kits
The how-to books with a twist: Each features projects and templates that will jumpstart your creativity, jog your imagination, and help you make the most of your Adobe software—fast! All the files you'll need are included on the accompanying disk, ready to be customized with your own artwork. You'll get fast, beautiful results without the learning curve.

Other Classics
Adobe Press books are the best way to go beyond the basics of your favorite Adobe application. Gain valuable insight and inspiration from well-known artists and respected instructors. Titles such as *The Complete Manual of Typography*, *Adobe Master Class: Design Invitational*, *Creating Acrobat Forms*, *Adobe Photoshop Web Design*, and *Photoshop One-Click Wow!* will put you on the fast track to mastery in no time.

The fastest, easiest, most comprehensive way to master Adobe Software

Visit www.adobepress.com for these titles and more!

Adobe Press